THE GREAT WAR ILLUSTRATED
1915

THE GREAT WAR ILLUSTRATED 1915

A Picture Editor's selection of 1,000 images illustrating historic events in 1915

William Langford & Jack Holroyd

Pen & Sword
MILITARY

*Dedicated to the One True Sovereign
who was disregarded by the nations when, in 1914, men elected to fight
among themselves on behalf of their own sovereignties*

First published in Great Britain in 2015 by
PEN & SWORD MILITARY
an imprint of
Pen & Sword Books Ltd,
47 Church Street, Barnsley,
South Yorkshire.
S70 2AS

Copyright © William Langford & Jack Holroyd, 2015

ISBN 978-1-47382-396-9

The right of William Langford & Jack Holroyd to be identified as Authors of this Work
has been asserted by them in accordance with the
Copyright, Designs and Patents Act 1988.

A CIP catalogue record for this book is available
from the British Library.

*All rights reserved. No part of this book may be reproduced or transmitted
in any form or by any means, electronic or mechanical including photocopying,
recording or by any information storage and retrieval system,
without permission from the Publisher in writing.*

Designed by Factionpress
Printed and bound in India by Replika Press Pvt. Ltd.

Pen & Sword Books Ltd incorporates the imprints of
Pen & Sword Aviation, Pen & Sword Maritime,
Pen & Sword Military, Pen & Sword Select, Pen & Sword Military Classics,
Leo Cooper, Wharncliffe Local History.

For a complete list of Pen & Sword titles please contact:
PEN & SWORD BOOKS LIMITED
47 Church Street, Barnsley, South Yorkshire, S70 2AS, England.
E-mail: enquiries@pen-and-sword.co.uk
Website: www.pen-and-sword.co.uk

Contents

	Introduction	6
Chapter One	**Losses and Gains – Fighting at Sea**	7
Chapter Two	**Middle East and the Gallipoli Failure**	47
Chapter Three	**The Battle of Neuve Chapelle**	145
Chapter Four	**The Second Battle of Ypres – Hill 60 – Gas**	167
Chapter Five	**Zeppelin Attack – Incentives to Join The Colours**	227
Chapter Six	**The New Army – The Armaments**	261
Chapter Seven	**The Battle of Loos**	311
	Index	363

The Taylor Picture Library

In 2002 publisher Charles Hewitt acquired the photographic archive of military collector and medals dealer, Peter N. Taylor of Barnsley, and in so doing instantly obtained thousands of potographs of both the First and Second World Wars. With this book, *The Great War Illustrated 1915*, a selection of over 1,000 images is displayed on its pages; an identification number has been given to the individual illustrations so that they may be ordered by authors, book designers, picture researchers and television and film programme makers. The images are all corrected and brought to the required specification and generous size requested by printers of books and magazines. The colour section has been produced by graphic designer Jon Wilkinson.

Peter Taylor has been dealing in medals and militaria for over twenty-five years, throughout which time he has had the foresight to buy up collections and albums of photographs, many of which were first generation press-release prints with an officially sanctioned caption on the back. In the eighties and nineties photographs of the Great War could be picked up for a few pence; now at arms fairs they may fetch up to £50 a print.

One hundred-year-old press release photographs may have incurred damage over time, such as the sample reproduced here of the hospital ship *Braemar Castle* preparing to leave Salonika. Present-day technology can bring about satisfactory restoration results that render an image suitable for reproduction. The example shown was heavily scratched, blistered, creased and faded out. A version of the same subject is shown below after it has been being worked on.

The *Braemar Castle* served in a variety of roles: as a cross-channel troop transport for the British Expeditionary Force in 1914; a troop transport in the Gallipoli campaign in 1915; and a hospital ship from 1915 onward. It was as a hospital ship in November 1916 that she struck a mine in the Aegean Sea, but was repaired. The attached picture label on the back reads:
ANOTHER HUN OUTRAGE ON THE RED CROSS
There is no atrocity too vile for the Huns to encompass, no outrage on Humanity's laws too fragrant to perpetrate. Close upon the sinking of the Britannic *hospital ship comes news that another stately liner, the* Braemar Castle, *bearing the sacred symbol of the Red Cross, has been 'mined or torpedoed' in the Aegean Sea. That all aboard, including homeward-bound wounded, are reported saved is a mercy that does not lesson the brutality of the crime. These photographs show the* Braemar Castle *ready to leave Salonica.*
FRENCH OFFICIAL WAR PHOTOGRAPH

Chapter One: Losses and Gains – Fighting at Sea, 1915

15GW003 The German armoured cruiser SMS *Blücher was* sunk in spectacular fashion on 24 January 1915 at the Battle of Dogger Bank.

15GW005 British 'bluejackets' loading a torpedo into its launching tube aboard a Royal Navy cruiser.

The year 1915 began with a shocking bang for the Royal Navy: it was in the early hours of the morning, 1 January, when a torpedo struck HMS *Formidable*, a pre-dreadnaught battleship. Part of the 5th Battle Squadron carrying out gunnery exercises off Portland, she was supported by the light cruisers *Topaze* and *Diamond*. Submarine activity had been reported in the area. *Formidable* was steaming at the rear of the squadron when a torpedo from U-24 struck the port side. The captain, Noel Loxley, gave the order to abandon ship. At about 03:05, *Formidable* was struck by a second torpedo on the starboard side. The two light cruisers came alongside and managed to pick up eighty men in the deteriorating weather. At 04:45 she rolled over onto men in the water and sank quickly. Captain Loxley remained on the bridge overseeing the evacuation of the ship. Loss of life was 35 officers (including Captain Loxley) and 512 men from a complement of 780. The Court of Inquiry found against Vice Admiral Sir Lewis Bayley, who had been in command of the squadron, as he had not taken precautions against the possibility of submarine attack. He was relieved of his command.

15GW006 HMS *Formidable* was sunk on the first day of January 1915 with the loss 512 men from a complement of 780. U-24 commander was Rudolf Schneider.

15GW007 Captain Noel Loxley, captain of the *Formidable*, stayed on the bridge and directed the evacuation of his crew. He went down with his ship.

15GW008 Some of the crew of the *Formidable* photographed after a coaling session.

"LASSIE"
THE FAMOUS DOG WHO SAVED THE LIFE OF COWAN
FROM H.M.S. FORMIDABLE.

15GW009 The original 'Lassie', who inspired films and a TV series, was a mongrel who saved the life of a sailor from HMS *Formidable*. Part collie, Lassie was owned by the landlord of a pub in Lyme Regis. On New Year's Day in 1915 the Royal Navy battleship *Formidable* was torpedoed by U-*24* off Start Point with heavy loss of life. A life raft containing bodies was swept along the coast to Lyme Regis. The corpses were retrieved and lodged in the pub cellar. Lassie made her way into the temporary mortuary, where she sought out and began to lick the face of one of the victims, Able Seaman John Cowan. She stayed beside him for more than half an hour, nuzzling him and keeping him warm with her body. Suddenly it was noted what she was doing and it was discerned that the 'dead' sailor was stirring. He was rushed to hospital and went on to make a full recovery. Cowan returned to thank all who saved his life – especially Lassie, who had sensed there was still life in him and worked hard to bring him back from the brink of death.

The sinking of the ship was a blow to Britain during these early years of the war and when it became known what Lassie had done, that inspirational and heart-warming story of Cowan's rescue was told again and again to any reporter who would listen. Hollywood eventually got a hold of the story and the rest is history.

15GW010 Loading a torpedo into the hold of a Royal Navy battleship.
15GW011 *Kapitänleutnant* Schneider. He was killed on 13 October 1917, in the North Sea.
15GW012 A German submarine, *U-21*, labouring through rough seas. It was conditions such as these off Portland on 1 January, that caused Admiral Sir Lewis Bayley to conclude there would be no likelihood of an attack by submarine. Two torpedos sank HMS *Formidable*.

15GW013 While sailing to join the 10th Cruiser Squadron, HMS *Viknor*, a requisitioned holiday cruiser, intercepted a Norwegian steamer carrying eight German passengers from the United States. These Germans were removed for internment in England. *Viknor* set a course for Liverpool to drop off the Germans and take on coal. She simply disappeared with all on board; twenty two officers, 237 ratings and the eight German nationals.

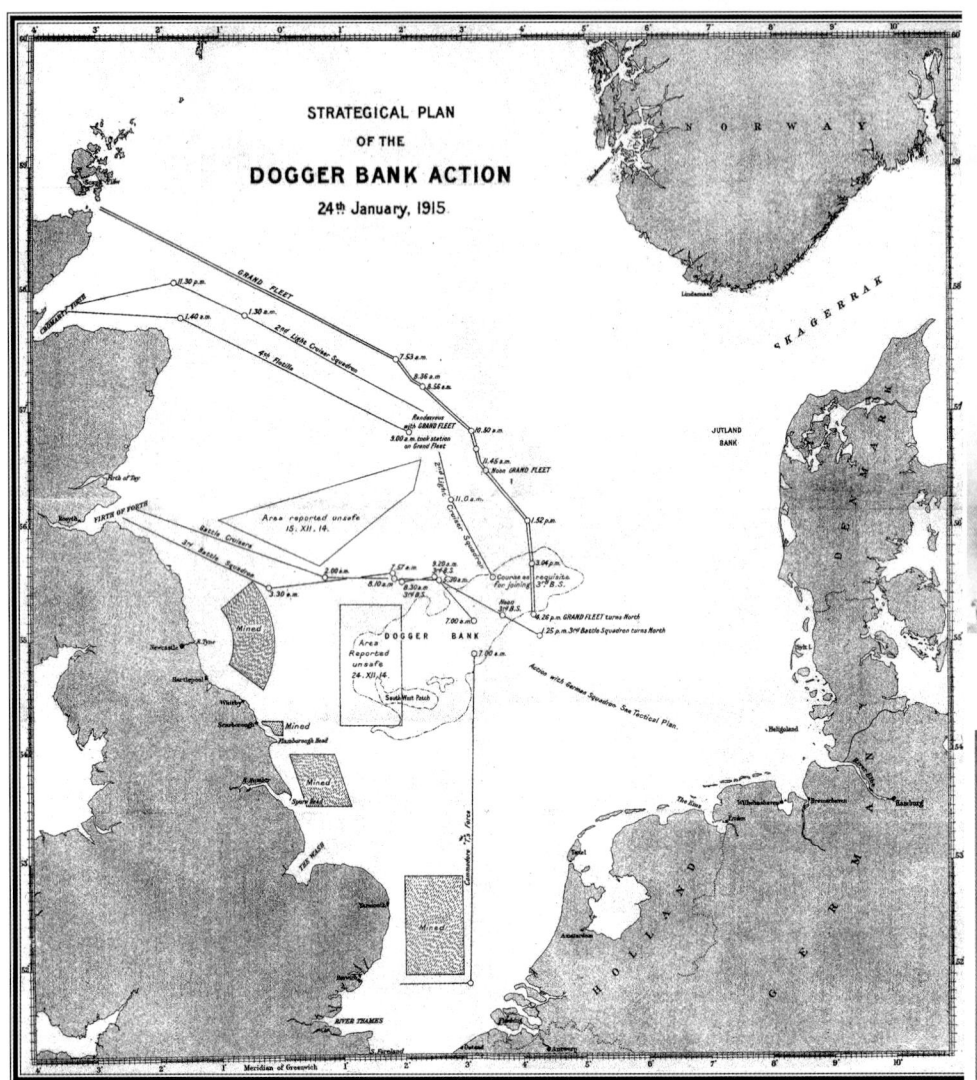

15GW015 Diagram showing the Dogger Bank action. Note the minefields defending Britain's East Coast.

15GW018 Artist's impression of the towing of the disabled HMS *Lion* by HMS *Indomitable*. Commissioned by *The Sphere* magazine and painted by Montague Dawson.

On 24 January a naval battle was fought near the Dogger Bank (a sandbank in a shallow area of the North Sea, about sixty miles off the east coast of England) between squadrons of the German High Seas Fleet and the Royal Navy's Grand Fleet. From decoded radio messages the British learned that a German raiding squadron was sailing for Dogger Bank. The British dispatched a force to intercept it. The Germans were caught by surprise and a chase lasting several hours ensued. The British caught up and engaged the slower moving Germans with long-range gunfire. The rear German ship, SMS *Blücher*, was hit but the British flagship, HMS *Lion*, was also hit and put out of action. Due to a signalling mixup, the remaining British ships broke off pursuit of the fleeing force to concentrate on sinking the *Blücher* and the German squadron escaped. The British flagship *Lion* made it back to port but was severely damaged. The action was considered a British victory, since they lost no ships and suffered few casualties, whereas the Germans lost a ship with most of its crew.

Both Britain and Germany replaced commanders who were thought to have shown poor judgement. Also numerous changes were made to procedures and equipment because of problems highlighted during the action.

15GW016 Vice Admiral Sir David Beatty.

15GW017 Franz Ritter von Hipper.

15GW014 Leading the attack on the German cruisers was HMS *Lion*. She was hit fourteen times and had taken aboard some water which gave her a list of ten degrees to port and reduced her speed. Shortly afterwards her port engine broke down and her speed dropped to 15 knots. Following the action, HMS *Indomitable* towed *Lion* back to port.

15GW019 SMS *Blücher* was at the rear of the German cruiser squadron at Dogger Bank and was caught by some long distance shooting by the British ships and was sunk.

15GW024 Royal Navy battle cruisers during the Battle of Dogger Bank receiving counter fire from the German ships. The photograph was taken from aboard one of the German ships.

15GW021 German sailors rescued from the *Blücher* marching to imprisonment in Edinburgh Castle.

15GW022 Capitain Alexander Karl Erdmann. SMS *Blücher*.

15GW020 SMS *Blücher* beginning the heel over. An impression of the event painted by an artist of *The Sphere* magazine.

15GW004 German sailors scramble for their lives as SMS *Blücher* rolls over before sinking.

15GW023 The funeral procession of Capitain Alexander Karl Erdmann of SMS *Blücher*. Following his rescue he died in Edinburgh Castle Hospital on 16 February 1915 and was given a funeral with full military honours. His flag-draped coffin, born on a gun carriage, is seen here proceeding to Dewington Cemetery. A guard of honour was provided by men of the 4th Battalion, the Royal Scots. There were some who questioned the arrangements, seeing as how Erdmann had taken part in the bombardment of the unfortified resort of Scarborough a few weeks' earlier.

15GW025 HMS *Lion* led the line in the chase after the German squadron at Dogger Bank. She was heavily damaged in an exchange of fire with SMS *Derfflinger* and had to be towed back to the base at Rosyth in Scotland.

15GW026 HMS *Princess Royal*, sister ship to the *Lion*, was launched at Barrow in 1911 and completed the following year. The photograph was taken during speed trials.

15GW027 HMS *Indomitable*, launched at Govan in 1907, was the first of her class of fast fighting ships which became known as 'battlecruisers'.

15GW028 HMS *Tiger*, clearly showing her tripod mast with housing for the fire-control instuments; the highest station on the ship is the Fire Directing position.

15GW031 Captain AEM Chatfield HMS *Lion*.

15GW033 Captain HB Pelly HMS *Tiger*.

15GW032 Captain O de B Brock HMS *Princess Royal*.

15GW030 Captain Lionel Halsey HMS *New Zealand*.

15GW034 Commodore R Tyrwhitt Destroyer flotilla.

15GW029 HMS *New Zealand*, built on the Clyde and launched in 1911, financed by a gift from the people of New Zealand.

1915

15GW035 Officers of HMS *Lion* with Vice-Admiral Sir David Beatty in the second row, seated, fifth from left. The *Lion* served as Vice Admiral Beatty's flagship at the Battle of Dogger Bank.

15GW036 The Signalling deck on HMS *Hampshire*. The semi-circle grid on the deck is to indicate the course the rest of the fleet is taking.

15GW037 The British Grand Fleet steaming in the North Sea, keeping guard on the East Coast.

15GW038 HMS *Bayano,* an armed merchant cruiser requisitioned from the Elders & Fyffes Line at the outbreak of war, was torpedoed and sunk off the coast of Scotland, 11 March 1915, by *U-27*, with the loss of 196 men.

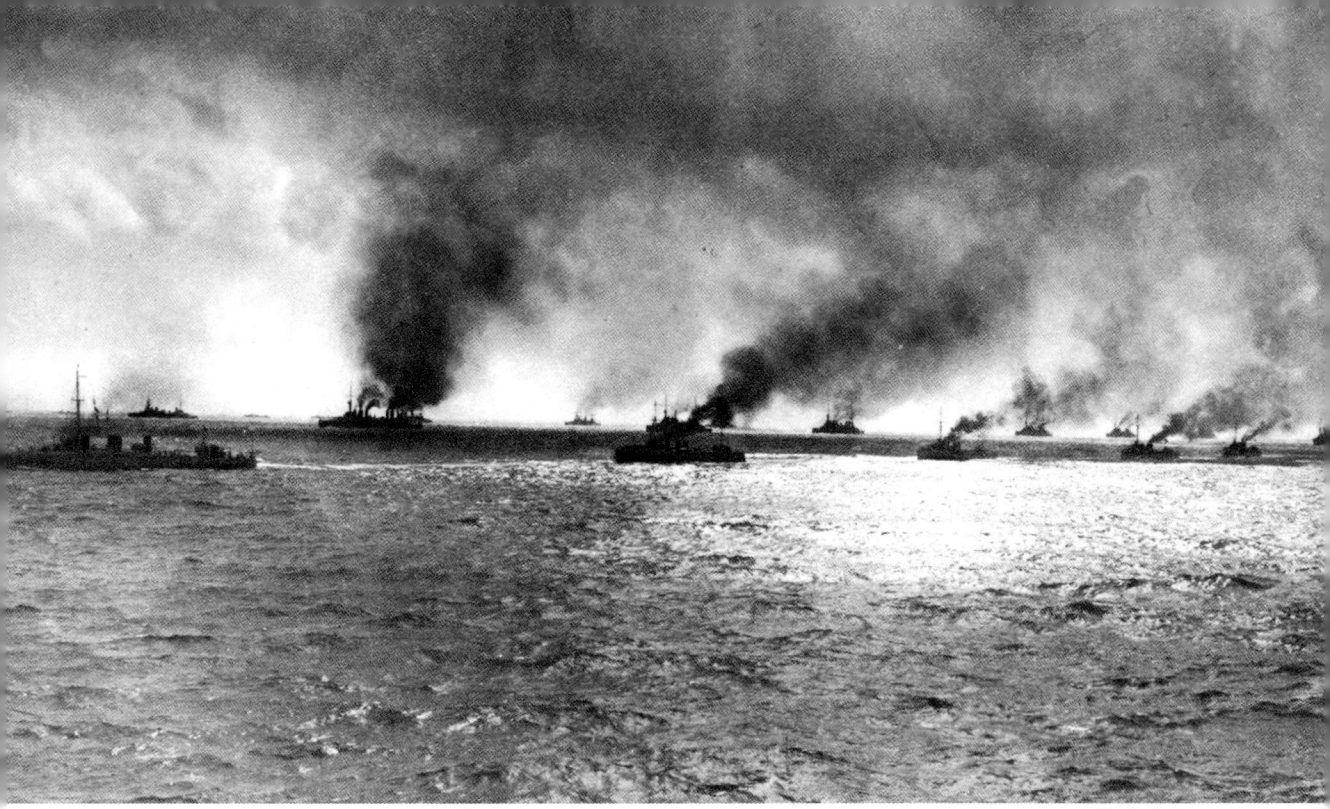

15GW039 British and French warships at the entrance to the Straits of the Dardanelles.

On 20 February 1915 the Secretary of the Admiralty made the following statements:
Yesterday [Friday] at 8 am a British fleet of battle-ships and battle-cruisers accompanied by flotillas, and aided by a strong French squadron, the whole under command of Vice-Admiral Sackville H Carden, began an attack upon the forts at the entrance to the Dardanelles.

This was followed five days later by a further statement:
The weather moderating, the bombardments of the out forts of the Dardanelles was renewed at 8 am this morning, 25 February. After a period of long-range fire, a squadron of battleships attacked at close range. All the forts at the entrance of the Straits have been successfully reduced.

Grand Duke Nicholas, commanding the Russian armies, had requested help against the Turks and the allied governments agreed to assist by attacking Turkey and by so doing relieve pressure on the Russians on the Caucasus front. The Dardanelles was selected as the place and a combined naval and military operation was planned. At first it was decided to attempt to force the straits by naval action alone, however, on 16 February the decision was modified, as it was agreed that the shores of the Dardanelles would have to be held. For this purpose a large military force under General Sir Ian Hamilton was assembled in Egypt. The French government also provided a military and naval contingent.

The planned naval bombardment began on the 16 February but was halted due to poor weather conditions and not resumed until over a week later. Demolition parties of marines landed almost unopposed, but bad weather again intervened. On 18 March the bombardment was continued. However, after three battleships had been sunk and three others damaged, the allied navies abandoned the attack, concluding that the fleet could not succeed without military help.

15GW041 Vice-Admiral Sir Sackville Hamilton Carden. He commanded the British fleet at the Dardanelles during the opening attack on the Turkish forts.

1915
17

15GW050 Loading naval shells for British cruisers. **15GW052** A British battle cruiser taking on shells for its main armament.

15GW047 The French battleship *Bouvet* steaming towards the Straits of the Dardanelles with other French ships of the squadron. After bombarding the forts she struck a mine while turning away. Out of her crew of 630 just sixty four were saved.

15GW051 A British battle cruiser taking on shells for its secondary armament.

15GW076 Taking ammuntion on board HMS *Agamemnon* for the Dardanelles fighting. The cylindrical containers hold cordite cartridges for the ship's 12-inch and 10-inch guns.

15GW070 The French cruiser *Henri IV*.

15GW046 A Royal Navy bluejacket and a French sailor, allies during the Dardanelles campaign.

15GW071 The Russian cruiser *Askold* joined the British and French fleets in the Dardanelles in a demonstration of Allied unity.

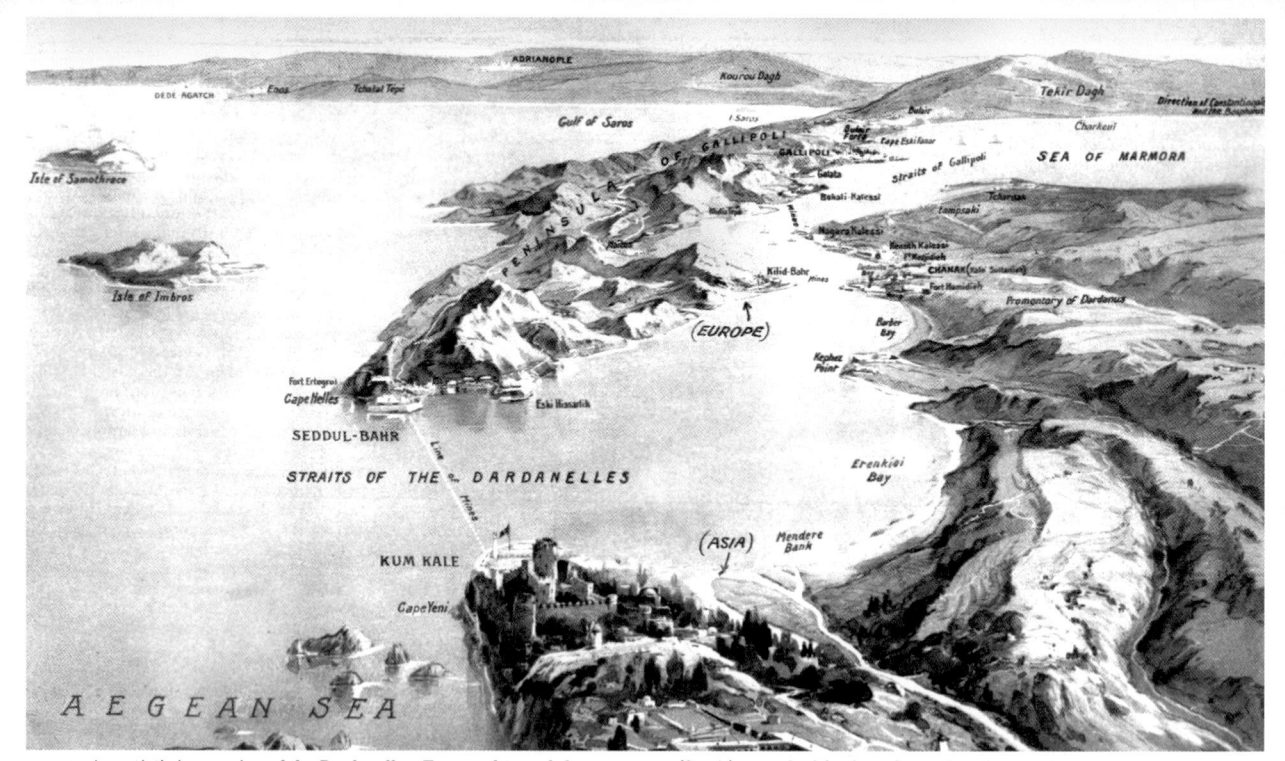

15GW072 An artist's impression of the Dardanelles. From end to end the water way (Strait) stretched for forty-five miles. Forts on both sides and minefields protected the Turkish territory where it formed a division between Asia and Europe.

15GW075 Entrance to the Straits of the Dardanelles with Turkish forts along both sides of the forty-five mile length – plus minefields.

15GW078 The Turkish town of Kilid Bahr where forts guarded the entrance to the Narrows fifteen miles into the Dardanelles.

15GW073 Commander of the British fleet engaged in forcing the Dardanelles, Vice Admiral Sackville Hamilton Carden, with his Flag-Lieutenant Lionel S. Ormsby-Johnson, strikes a commanding pose for the camera in front of Admiralty House, Malta.

Vice Admiral Sackville Hamilton Carden's plan for the naval action required the systematic destruction of Turkish fortifications along the Dardanelles while advancing slowly up the strait, with minesweepers leading the way. Carden was successful in early offensives against the Turkish defenses from February until early March, when he was relieved of command due to his failing health and replaced by Admiral John de Robeck.

15GW074 Admiral Sir John de Robeck.

15GW054 A street scene in the Ottoman town of Dardanelle from which the Straits take their name.

15GW055 Turkish troops

15GW079 A Turkish fort protecting the Straits of the Dardanelles shortly before the Allied bombardment.

1915

15GW080 Turkish battery of German supplied 77 mm field guns overlooking the Straits of the Dardanelles.

15GW081 A Turkish fort protecting the Dardanelles shortly before the Allied bombardment, March 1915.

15GW086 British cruisers heading towards the Turkish homeland with a view to forcing the Dardanelles and reaching Constantinople (Istanbul). The intention was to knock Turkey out of the war by capturing the capital city.

15GW077 Decks cleared for action on a British cruiser: bulwark rails have been lowered; all deck gear has been removed and the decks sluiced with water.

15GW083 Ottoman artillery observers spotting for the field guns supporting the static defences of the Dardanelles forts.

15GW053 HMS *Triumph* steaming in line into the Dardanelle Straits with other Allied warships prior to the bombardment of Turkish forts.

1915

15GW087 Stokers work hard at feeding the ship's boilers on a Royal Navy cruiser. 
15GW056 British and French cruisers shelling the Turkish forts.
15GW043 HMS *Cornwallis* bombarding the Ottoman forts on 18 March 1915.

On 19 February 1915 two British destroyers were sent to probe the defences of the Dardanelles. The Ottomans opened fire from Kumkale with the Orhaniye Tepe battery's 240 mm (9.4 in) Krupp guns at 07.58. The battleships HMS *Cornwallis* and *Vengeance* moved in to engage the forts and the first British shots of the campaign proper were fired at 09.51 by the *Cornwallis*.

15GW042, 15GW058, 15GW059 British and French cruisers shelling Turkish forts with their main armament and secondary armaments.

15GW049 Smoke arising from the Ottoman forts as shells from bombarding allied ships explode on target.

1915
25

15GW088 French cruiser *Bouvet* ran onto a mine as she was leaving the firing line during the bombardment of the Ottoman forts and sank very quickly.

15GW089 French cruiser *Suffren* took part in the bombardment of the Ottoman batteries at Suandere and Mount Dardanos.

15GW090 French cruiser *Gaulois* took part in the bombardment of the Ottoman batteries at Suandere and Mount Dardanos.

15GW091 The French cruiser *Bouvet* ran onto a mine during course changes while shelling the Ottoman forts and sank very quickly with a high loss of life.

15GW092 HMS *Irresistible* one of four British battleships chosen to take part in the attempt to force the narrows on 18 March 1915 (along with *Ocean*, *Vengeance*, *Albion* and *Irresistible*). She was taking part in a bombardment of Turkish forts at a distance of 11,000 yards. She was drifting with her engines stopped and ran onto a mine. The engine room flooded and only three men escaped. The pressure of in-running water created pressure that broke down the midship bulkhead and the port engine-room also flooded. The ship was listing at seven degrees, with her stern down and the engine gone. She then came under heavy Turkish fire. Captain Dent ordered the crew to abandon ship. Despite being under heavy fire, the destroyer HMS *Wear* rescued 28 officers and 582 men from the *Irresistible*. An attempt to get her under tow by HMS *Ocean* failed and she was abandoned. After that she drifted back under the guns of the Turkish forts and was sunk by gunfire.

15GW044 HMS *Irresistible*, sinking after coming under shell fire from Turkish forts. The destroyer *Ocean* took off 610 officers and men. She was continually pounded until sunk, providing excellent target practice for the defending Turkish gunners.

The Turkish forces defending the sea approaches to their capital city Constantinople and entrance to the Black Sea, must have been elated when they had a grandstand view of three attacking cruisers going to the bottom in quick succession.

15GW093 HMS *Ocean* was one of the bombarding ships targeting the Ottoman forts in the Dardanelles when, after assisting the stricken *Irresistible*, she also struck a mine and, after receiving shell fire from the land batteries, sank. Her crew was saved.

15GW095 On board a British warship off the Dardanelles. A party of sailors about to set off for the bombarded Turkish coast forts; a party of Marines, on the left, prepare to give support.

15GW098 Turkey's gallant defence – the minelayer *Nusret* sowed mines with great effectiveness in defending the approaches to Istanbul.

15GW094 HMS *Amethyst*, a British Light Cruiser, managed to cruise the length of the narrows as far as the town of Nagara. She came under sustained fire along the way. The number of her crew killed amounted to twenty eight with thirty wounded.

15GW065 A British shore party makes an unopposed landing in the Dardanelles. It was inevitable that Sedd-el Bahr, positioned at the gateway to the Dardanelles Straits, would be attacked at the outset. After intense shelling, sailors and marines landed on 26 February 1915 to finish what the ships' guns had started, using demolition charges.

Royal Marine landing parties found wrecked Turkish forts and streets, which gave evidence of the ferocious barrage unleashed from French and British warships off shore.

15GW067 The Fortress at Sedd-el Bahr reduced by the guns of HMS *Queen Elizabeth*.

15GW066 A marine sentry guards a broken gate in the Turkish defences.

15GW060 The streets of Sedd-el Bahr cleared of rubble after the naval shelling.

15GW061 A destroyed Turkish gun, put out of action during the bombardment.

15GW062 Big guns of this fort were rendered useless by shells blowing them out of their carriage.

15GW063 A painted slogan calling upon Allah for his favour decorates this gun equipment.

15GW064 A Turkish howitzer blown

1915
31

15GW137 British marines taking cover during their landings on Turkish soil and operations against the villages of Sedd-el Bahr, Kum Kale and Yeni Shehr.

15GW148 Royal Marines, part of the Dardanelles landing party, try out firing positions in a Turkish fort.

15GW149 British marines passing through the streets of a Turkish village.

15GW152 British marines ashore on the island of Tenedos.

15GW150 Marines at drill by the Turkish fort at Sedd-ul-Bahr and seemingly making a mess of performing 'right shoulder arms' in front of some locals.

15GW153 Royal Marines keeping guard over a Turkish town and its obsolete fortress. The fortress is surrounded by sea on three sides and by a moat on the landward approaches

15GW102 His Majesty's Submarine *E1*, the first of its class.

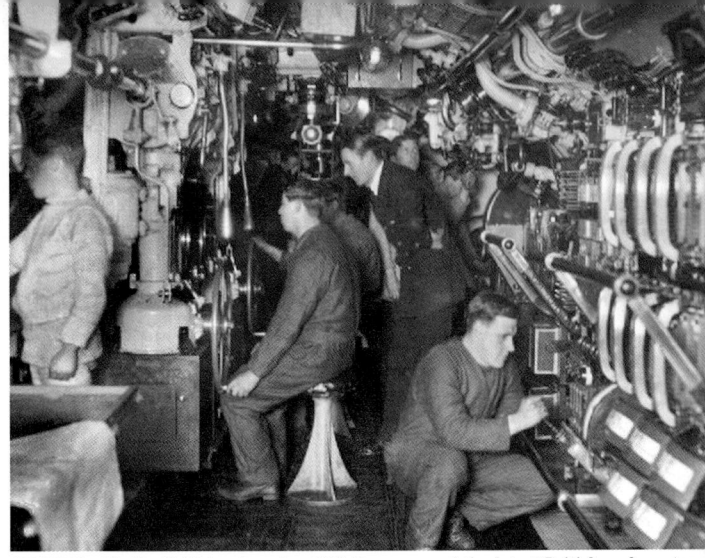

The *E15* was the first British submarine to attempt a passage of the Dardanelles. It got caught in a cross current and ran aground near Kephez Point on the Asian shore under the guns of a Turkish shore battery. The Captain, Commander Brodie, was killed in the coning tower and six others died of chlorine poisoning inside the submarine. The rest of the crew became prisoners of war. The *E15* was one of the latest British submarines and the Royal Navy went to great lengths to stop it remaining intact in enemy hands. After numerous attempts to destroy it by the Royal Navy, HMS *Majestic* finally succeeded.

15GW097 Inside the British submarine *E15*. It was one of the latest British underwater craft and was operating in the Dardanelles when it ran aground.

Royal Navy submarine *E14*, off Lemnos, Greece, 1915. Under the command of Lieutenant Commander Edward Boyle, it made three sorties through the defences of the Dardanelles in 1915. During one of them he sank a Turkish minelayer, a gunboat, a transport ship and damaged another transport. On 18 May, Boyle brought the submarine back safely through the Dardanelles.

15GW099 Navy submarine *E14*, somewhere at sea near Gallipoli in May 1915. For his successful patrol of the Dardanelles and the Sea of Marmora in April-May 1915, Boyle was awarded the Victoria Cross. His VC citation reads:

For most conspicuous bravery, in command of Submarine E14, when he dived his vessel under enemy minefields and entered the Sea of Marmara on 27 April, 1915. In spite of great navigational difficulties from strong currents, of the continual neighbourhood of hostile patrols, and of the hourly danger of attack from the enemy, he continued to operate in the narrow waters of the Straits and succeeded in sinking two Turkish gunboats and one large military transport. [The London Gazette, 21 May 1915]

15GW105 Crew of the Royal Australian Navy's Submarine *AE2*. In April 1915, on the day of the landings at Gallipoli, the *AE2* entered the Sea of Marmara but was spotted by a Turkish torpedo boat, the *Sultan Hisa*, and attacked. Lieutenant Henry Stoker, *AE2*'s captain, scuttled the submarine when it became uncontrollable. There was no loss of life and the crew became prisoners of war in Turkey.

15GW096 On 17 April 1915, submarine *E15*, under the command of Lieutenant Commander Theodore Brodie, ran aground under the guns of a Turkish shore battery. The *E15* is seen here being inspected by Turkish soldiers and sailors. The submarine was eventually destroyed by gunfire from HMS *Majestic* to avoid its further examination and possible future use by the Central Powers.

15GW100 Lieutenant Commander Edward Boyle VC, on the deck of the *E14*, somewhere in the Mediterranean.

15GW101 Lieutenant Commander Edward Boyle VC.

15GW104 Turkish postcard commemorating the victory of the *Sultan Hisa* over the Australian submarine *AE2*.

15GW103 The *AE2*; Lieutenant Henry Stoker, *AE2*'s captain, scuttled her when the boat became uncontrollable during evasive action.

15GW106 HMS *Goliath*; with the Gallipoli landings being carried out on the Turkish mainland, Royal Navy and French major ships were involved in a constant bombardment of the shore in support of the attacks.

On 12-13 May, HMS *Goliath* was anchored in Morto Bay off Cape Helles when, an hour after midnight, the Turkish torpedo boat *Muâvenet-i Millîye*, eluded the destroyers HMS *Beagle* and HMS *Bulldog* and closed in on the battleship. *Muâvenet-i Millîye* fired two torpedoes that struck *Goliath* close to her fore turret and abeam the fore funnel, causing a massive explosion. *Goliath* began to capsize when a third torpedo struck near the after turret. She then rolled over completely and began to sink by the bows, taking 570 of the 750-strong crew down, including her captain, Thomas Lawrie Shelford. The torpedo boat slipped away without being spotted by the two defending destroyers.

5GW108 HMS *Triumph*, with her anti-submarine torpedo nets in place. These failed to prevent a torpedo striking the battleship amidship. The periscope of the German submarine had been spotted and was fired upon. The escorting destroyer, HMS *Chelmer*, tried to ram the submarine but failed, and despite watertight doors on the battleship being closed the ship gradually rolled over and after thirty minutes sank. HMS *Chelmer* managed to lift many of the crew off before *Triumph* sank. Over seventy men went down with the ship.

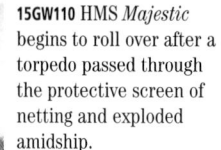

15GW110 HMS *Majestic* begins to roll over after a torpedo passed through the protective screen of netting and exploded amidship.

15GW112 *Kapitänleutnant* Otto Hersing, commander of *U-21*, sank two Royal Navy battleships in a matter of a few days.

15GW107 HMS *Triumph* was engaged in shore bombardment off Gaba Tepe, Gallipoli, when the German submarine *U.21*, under the command of Captain Hersing, launched a torpedo, striking her amidship. Seventy-three officers and men died.

15GW109 HMS *Majestic* was stationed off W Beach at Cape Helles when she became the third battleship to be torpedoed off the Gallipoli peninsula in two weeks. On 27 May 1915, at 0645 hours, Commander Otto Hersing of *U-21* fired a single torpedo through the screen of destroyers and torpedo nets, killing 49 men.

15GW114 Looking towards the aft torpedo tube in a German World War One submarine.

15GW113 Inside a German submarine, an officer using the boat's periscope.

15GW111 German submarine *U-21*.

1915
37

15GW1120 RMS *Lusitania* under attack from *U-20* as depicted on a German postcard. The German submarine went on to sink another liner, RMS *Hesperian*.

15GW1121 The liner RMS *Hesperian* was sunk by *U-20* shortly after the *Lusitania*.

15GW1122 Torpedo tubes on the *U-20* type German submarine.

15GW1123 Artist's impression of the *U-20* type receiving a salute from some capitol ships of the German High Seas Fleet.

15GW117 RMS *Lusitania* was launched on 7 June 1906.

15GW115 RMS *Lusitania*, sailing into New York, was the holder of the Blue Riband and briefly the world's biggest ship.

15GW119 *Lusitania* at the end of the first leg of her maiden voyage, New York City, September 1907.

15GW120 *Lusitania* arriving at Liverpool and completing her maiden voyage.

15GW116 First Class Dining room aboard the *Lusitania*.

15GW118 RMS *Lusitania* entering New York Harbour under the control of tug boats.

15GW121 RMS *Lusitania* heading into the Atlantic under full steam. She was fitted with revolutionary new turbine engines, able to maintain a speed of 25 knots. Equipped with lifts, wireless telegraph and electric light, she provided 50% more passenger space than any other ship, whilst the first class decks were noted for their sumptuous furnishings.

1915
41

15GW124 RMS *Lusitania* docking and being greeted by crowds.

15GW129 and 138a RMS *Lusitania* receiving a grey paint job to her funnels and bridge to make her less conspicuouse to prowling German submarines.

15GW122 Captain of the *Lusitania*, William Turner 'Bowler Bill', was one the Cunard Line's most respected captains. He stayed at his post throughout the sinking and stayed with the ship until she sank under him.

15GW130 RMS *Lusitania* heads out into the Atlantic ocean and her meeting with destiny.

15GW126 On the afternoon of 7 May, *Lusitania* was torpedoed by a submarine eleven miles off the southern coast of Ireland. She sank in eighteen minutes.

CUNARD

OCEAN STEAMSHIPS.

EUROPE VIA LIVERPOOL
LUSITANIA
Fastest and Largest Steamer
now in Atlantic Service Sails
SATURDAY, MAY 1, 10 A. M.
Transylvania, Fri., May 7, 5 P.M.
Orduna, - - Tues.,May 18, 10 A.M.
Tuscania, - - Fri., May 21, 5 P.M.
LUSITANIA, Sat., May 29, 10 A.M.
Transylvania, Fri., June 4, 5 P.M.

Gibraltar-Genoa-Naples-Piraeus
S.S. Carpathia, Thur., May 13, Noon

NOTICE!
TRAVELLERS intending to embark on the Atlantic voyage are reminded that a state of war exists between Germany and her allies and Great Britain and her allies; that the zone of war includes the waters adjacent to the British Isles; that, in accordance with formal notice given by the Imperial German Government, vessels flying the flag of Great Britain, or of any of her allies, are liable to destruction in those waters and that travellers sailing in the war zone on ships of Great Britain or her allies do so at their own risk.

IMPERIAL GERMAN EMBASSY
WASHINGTON, D. C. APRIL 22, 1915.

Germany had declared the seas around the United Kingdom to be a war zone, and the German embassy in the United States had placed a newspaper advertisement warning people not to sail on the *Lusitania*. On the afternoon of 7 May, *Lusitania* was torpedoed by a German submarine, eleven miles off the southern coast of Ireland and inside the declared 'zone of war'. A second internal explosion sent her to the bottom in eighteen minutes.

In firing on a non-military ship without warning, the Germans had breached the international laws known as the Cruiser Rules. However, the Germans had reasons for treating *Lusitania* as a naval vessel, the ship was carrying war munitions and the British had also been breaching the Cruiser Rules. The sinking caused a storm of protest in the United States and influenced the decision by the US to declare war in 1917.

15GW123 On April 22, 1915, the German Embassy had issued a warning to Great Britain and her allies travelling overseas.

15GW132/15GW142a/15GW142b Survivors from the sinking of the *Lusitania*.

15GW131 *Kapitänleutnant* Walther Schwieger commander of *U-20* which sank the *Lusitania*.

15GW125 German propaganda postcard celebrating the sinking of the *Lusitania*.

1915

15GW143a A survivor, still wearing his life-preserver, was labelled a 'cripple' on the original caption.

15GW143d Two brothers named Gardener who survived the sinking; the youngest is being helped by a hotel porter and supported by his elder brother.

15GW143b This young couple, Miss B William and Mr J Lane, have just stepped from the rescue boat. They have been provided with warm, over-sized top coats.

15GW139 Five of the ship's lifeboats which landed survivors from the *Lusitania* at Queenstown Harbour. Some local children seize the opportunity to explore the boats. One can be seen trying on a life preservrr.

15GW141 A dead American citizen, killed when the German submarine *U-20* attacked and sank the *Lusitania*, is carried through the streets of the Irish port of Queensland. It was hoped that images such as this would influence American public opinion and prompt President Wilson to declare war on Germany.

15GW142c Captain of the RMS *Lusitania*, William Thomas Turner, OBE, RNR (October 23, 1856 – June 23, 1933) was rescued from the sea.

15GW127 A propaganda opportunity for home and foreign press. The main staged ingredients were: a baby, a dead parent; and the heavily painted name on the lifeboat. Compare the latter with the lettering on the lifeboats opposite.

15GW142d A funeral procession at Queensland, Ireland, for victims of the RMS *Lusitania*, 10 May, 1915.

15GW142e A mass grave at Queensland, Ireland, for victims of the RMS *Lusitania*.

Chapter Two: Middle East and the Gallipoli failure

15GW155 An Ottoman gun crew ready for action. The Turks would fight fiercely to defend their homeland from the invading French and British.

15GW154 British and Australian troops on the deck of a battlecruiser, preparing to take to long boats for landings at Gallipoli.

15GW157 The Suez Canal is a 101 mile long waterway that connects the Mediterranean Sea with the Gulf of Suez. It officially opened in November 1869.

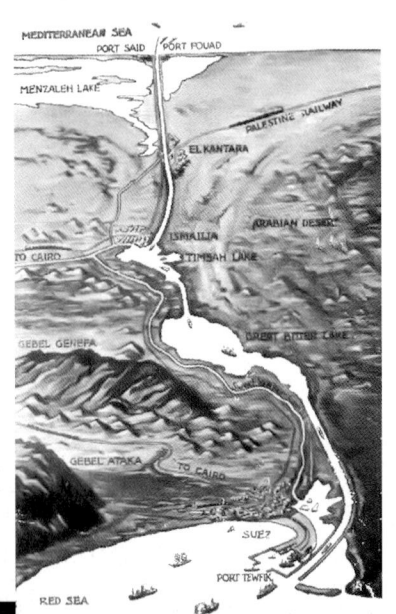

After ten years of construction work the Suez Canal opened in November 1869. It allowed ships to sail between Europe and eastern Asia without having to navigate around Africa. The northern terminus is Port Said and the southern terminus is Port Tawfiq, at the city of Suez.

In 1856, Frenchman Ferdinand de Lesseps obtained a concession from the Khedive of Egypt and Sudan to construct a canal open to ships of all nations. A company was formed and was to operate the canal for ninety-nine years from its opening. The canal had an immediate and dramatic effect on world trade.

The canal was declared a neutral zone under the protection of the British, who had occupied Egypt and Sudan at the request of Khedive Tewfiq to suppress the Urabi Revolt against his rule.
The British army in the First World War undertook the defence of the canal and had to defend the strategically important passage against a major Ottoman attack in 1915.

Ferdinand Marie, Vicomte de Lesseps
(19 November 1805–7 December 1894).

15GW158 Ships sailing through the Suez Canal were vulnerable to attack from Turkish forces, who had mounted an incursion at the end of January 1915.

15GW160 A screen of rushes erected on the mail-steamer *Ville de la Ciotat* to mask the crew from Turkish snipers along the banks of the canal.

15GW162 Banks of the Suez Canal where the Turks sought to cross. Along its length the canal is 65 yards wide and 29 feet deep.

15GW172 A photograph that appeared in a German journal, showing their interest in this strategic waterway.

15GW163 An Indian Army Maxim section on the banks of the Suez Canal.

15GW184 An artist's impression of how the attack on the Suez Canal was repelled.

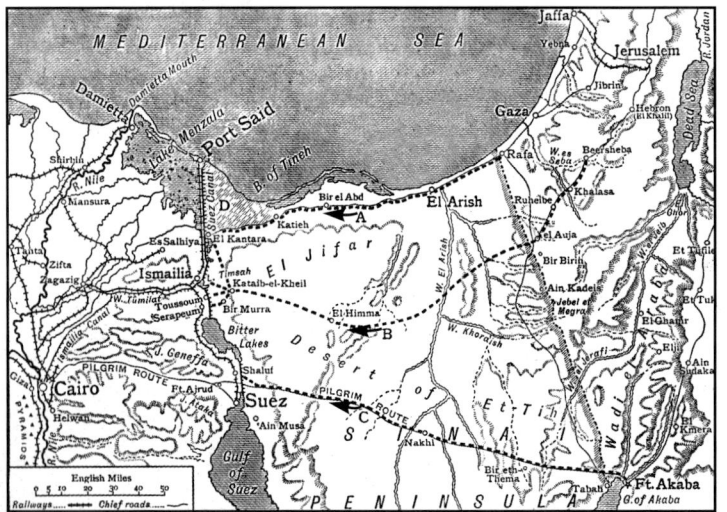

15GW169 A damaged pontoon brought up to the Canal by the Turks for crossing the water – manufactured in Germany.

15GW170 Map of three-pronged attack on the Suez Canal by the Turks, 25 January–3 February 1915.
A: Route of small force attacking at El Kantara.
B: Advance from Beersheba to Kataib-el-Kheil and the main attack.
C: A small force used the road known as the Pilgrim Route for an attack north of Suez.

15GW197 Turkish troops muster on the Plain of Esdraelon before the attack on the Suez Canal, 1915.

15GW196 Lieutenant General Sir John Grenfell Maxwell, commander of the forces defending the Suez Canal.

15GW164 A German postcard depicting their version of the raid on the Canal by their allies, the Turks.

15GW284 Men of the New Zealand Brigade after landing in Egypt.
15GW283 Pack mules panicking after a platoon of British infantry, with bayonets fixed, crosses their path among the dunes in Egypt.

15GW281 New Zealanders of the New Zealand and Australian Division, part of ANZAC, taking a break in Egypt.

1915
53

15GW286 A column of the New Zealand and Australian Division on the march in Egypt.
15GW282 Bird's eye view of a part of an Allied camp in Egypt.

15GW280 A change of mounts for these men of a British cavalry regiment.
15GW285 Battalion cooks of the New Zealand Brigade preparing the evening meal.

15GW198 *Generalleutnant* Otto Liman von Sanders served as an adviser and military commander for the Ottoman Empire.

15GW192 German scout biplane over Egypt.

15GW168 A Turkish light artillery unit equipped with a Krupps 77 mm field gun.

15GW199 Kress von Kressenstein, commander of the First Suez Offensive in January 1915.

15GW173 Port Said, situated at the entrance to the Suez Canal and target for the Turkish invaders.

15GW165 Turkish infantry in the Sinai Desert, posing a threat to the Suez Canal.

15GW181 A Turkish light artillery unit, with their gun disassembled and packed onto mules.

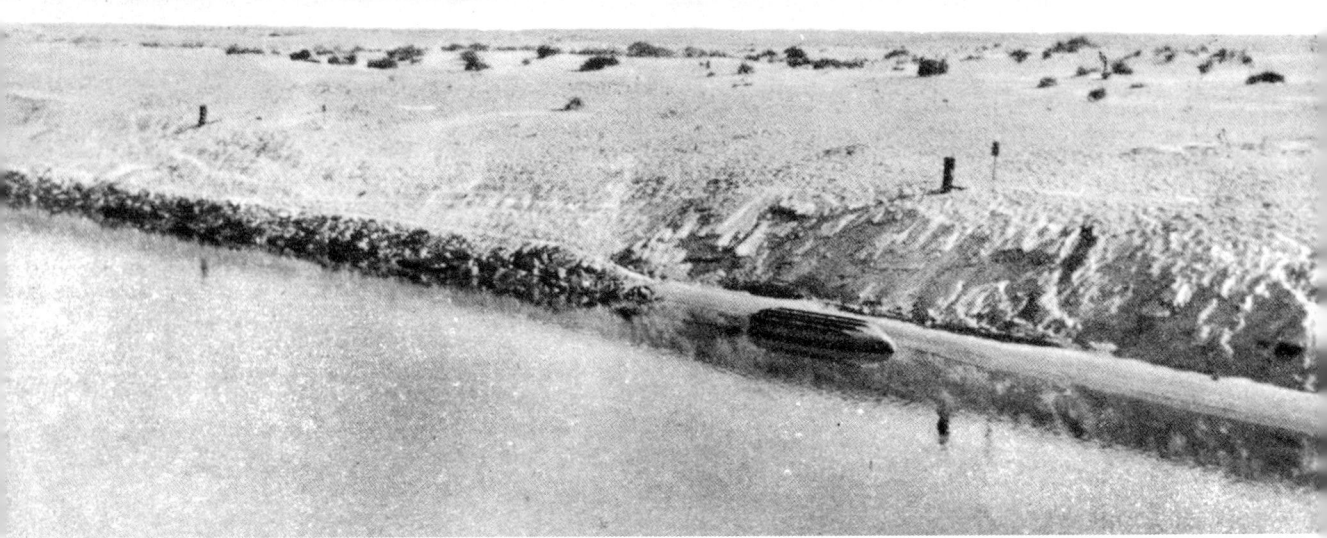

15GW166 An overturned boat on the eastern bank of the Canal marks the spot where Turkish forces sought to cross between 25 January and 3 February 1915.

15GW161 Turkish prisoners held in temporary cages aboard a Royal Navy warship.

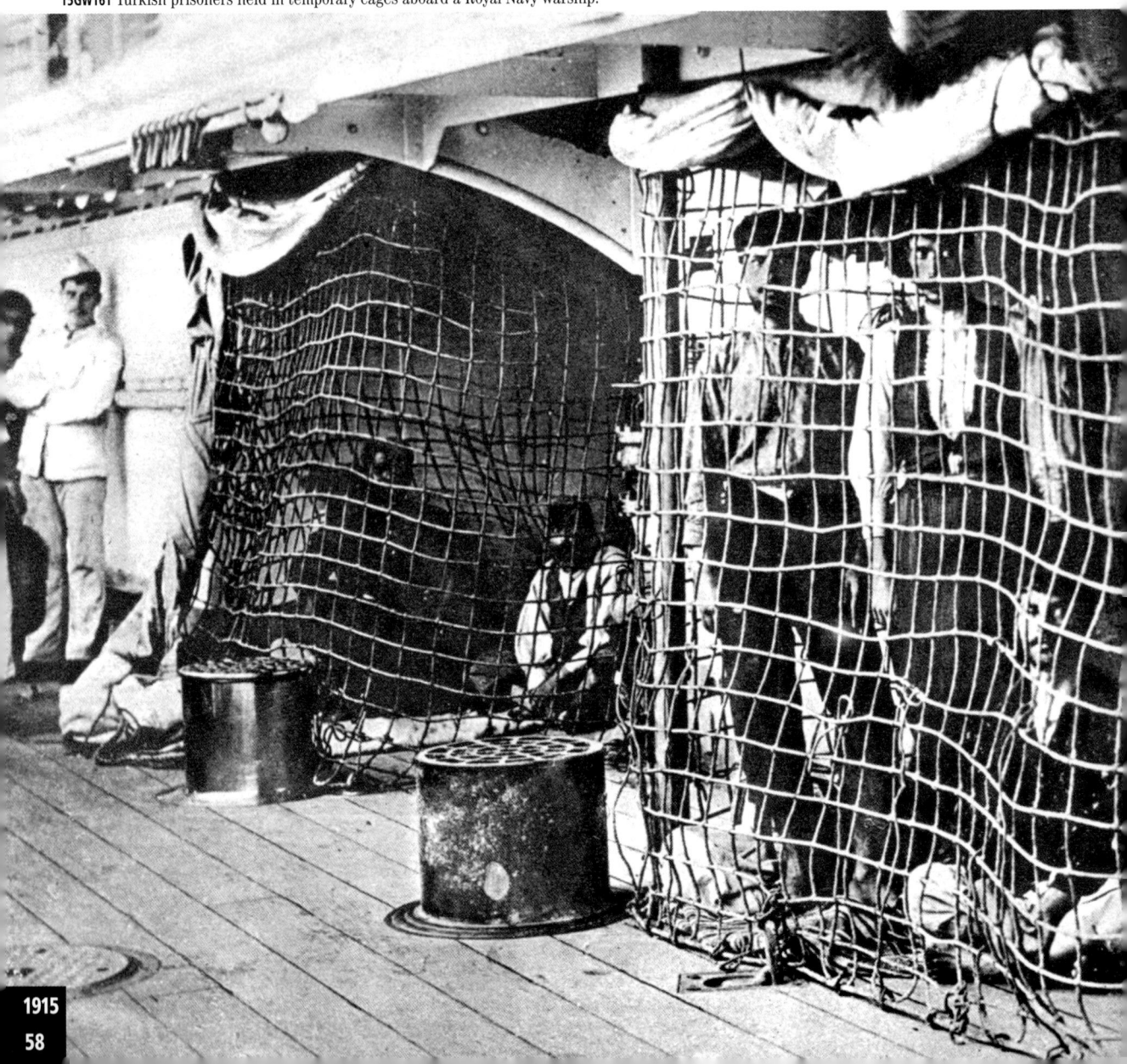

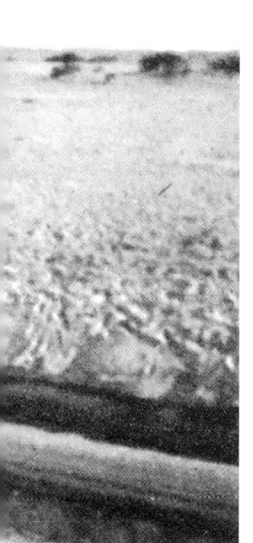

15GW171 Turkish prisoners taken during the abortive raid on the Suez Canal are marched into Cairo.

15GW176 Turkish infantry.

15GW178 Turkish marines.

15GW200 The Sultan of Turkey leaves his palace in Constantinople.

15GW189 Turkish soldiers assembled outside the Sultan's palace in Constantinople.

15GW190 Turkish infantry.

15GW167 Rallying to the flag: Reservists march up to join the colours while uniformed soldiers set out to meet the invaders of their country.

15GW203 A Turkish spotter plane, built in Germany.

15GW201 Wilhelm Freiherr von der Goltz, German Vice President of the Turkish Military Council.

15GW187 Turkish artillery moving out of the capital to battle with the British and French invaders.

15GW202 The Turkish heir to the throne with his staff on an inspection tour of Gallipoli.

1915
61

15GW205 An Austrian howitzer being inspected by Enver Pasha (right, with sword).
15GW204 Turkish artillery equipped with a Krupp 77 mm field gun.

15GW227 Turks crossing from Constantinople to the Asiatic shore away from the threatened city.

15GW183 A platoon of Turkish infantry with its officer.

With German guidance, the Turks were prepared to repel a landing on either side of the peninsula and were employing five divisions and with another division en route, (a conscript force, commanded by Otto Liman von Sanders). The Ottoman military commanders along with senior German officers planned the defence for the anticipated landing. They all agreed that the most effective form of defence was to hold the high ground on the ridges of the peninsula and, because of the British delay, they had four weeks in which to prepare a hot reception.

15GW194 Liman von Sanders and the Duke of Mecklenburg-Schwerin being driven to inspect the Turkish positions.

15GW177 The finer points of the German Mauser rifle being demonstrated to a group of Turkish soldiers who have just been equipped with the weapon.

15GW182 A Turkish commanding officer of an infantry battalion with his officers.

15GW1780 Two gun crew demonstrating the correct – though precarious – travelling position when moving a German 77 mm field gun.

15GW185 Turkish infantry file into a trench at Gallpoli.

15GW186 Awaiting the British onslaught at Gallpoli.

15GW191 Admiral De Roebeck and General Sir Ian Hamilton at Gallpoli.

15GW210 An artist's drawing of the Gallpoli Peninsula and the Asiatic shore.

The Dardanelles provided a sea route to Russia, ally of Britain and France, and those nations launched a naval attack followed by an amphibious landing on the peninsula with the goal of capturing the Ottoman capital of Constantinople. On 25 April landings were made at six beaches on the peninsula. The British 29th Division landed at Helles on the tip of the peninsula and were to then advance upon the forts at Kilitbahir. The Australians and New Zealanders (Anzacs), with the 3rd (Australian) Infantry Brigade spearheading the assault, were to land north of Gaba Tepe, from where they could advance across the peninsula, cutting off the Ottoman troops in Kilitbahir. The small cove in and around which they landed became known as 'Anzac Cove'.

15GW207 Australian soldiers cheer the French as they are about to sail for the Gallpoli Peninsula.

15GW208 French troops waiting to embark for a diversionary landing at Kum Kale, on the Asiatic side of the Straits.

15GW211 British troops leaving a Royal Navy ship for the assault

15GW209 Sub-Lieutenant Rupert Chawner Brooke, English poet, died 23 April 1915 aged 27. He sailed with the British Mediterranean Expeditionary Force on 28 February 1915. On his way to the landing at Gallipoli he developed sepsis from an infected mosquito bite and died aboard a French hospital ship moored off the island of Skyros in the Aegean.

> *If I should die, think only this of me:*
> *That there's some corner of a foreign field*
> *That is for ever England.*
>
> Rupert Brooke

15GW365 Royal Navy pilots and observers tasked with flying over Gallipoli and taking photographs prior to the landings.

15GW366 Wing Commander C.R. Samson, an RNAS pilot alongside his Nieuport scout. He is holding an automatic pistol.

15GW367 The town of Gallipoli taken from a British aircraft. The town was one of the objectives of the invading force en route to the capture of the Ottoman capital city, Constantinople.

15GW319 German naval officers and men wearing Turkish naval uniforms and insignia. The German warships SMS *Breslau* and SMS *Goeben* were passed to the Turkish navy, joining SMS *Kurfürst Friedrich Wilhelm*, which had been sold to them pre-war. With these ships the Turks were able to attack the Russian Black Sea Fleet, merchant shipping and port installations.

15GW368 Constantinople harbour, where Turkish warships lie anchored. The view is from Pera looking towards the capital. The ship with four funnels is the German cruiser *Breslau* and the one to the right is the Turkish battleship *Barbaros Hayreddin* (formerly SMS *Kurfürst Friedrich*).

15GW370 Ex-German cruiser *Breslau* – renamed *Midilli*.

15GW369 Ex-German battleship *Kurfürst Friedrich Wilhelm* was sold to the Ottoman Empire and renamed *Barbaros Heyreddin*.

15GW363 French troops on the Greek island of Lemnos – the jumping off point for the Gallipoli landings.

15GW364 Australian troops march into tented accommodation on Lemnos.

15GW371 A church service aboard a British warship before the Gallipoli landings. The band is situated between the two gun barrels. The chaplain, standing next to the captain, conducts the service '... a few brief prayers are said, a brief extract from the Bible is read, the blessing pronounced, and all is over'.

15GW372 Allied camaraderie at the Dardenelles: Admiral Roebuck introduces Admiral Nicholson to General General Gouraud and General D'Amade.

'SOLDIERS OF FRANCE AND OF THE KING

Before us lies an adventure unprecedented in modern war. Together with our comrades of the fleet we are about to force a landing upon an open beach in face of positions which have been vaunted by our enemies as impregnable. The landing will be made good by the help of God and the Navy; the positions will be stormed and the war brought one step nearer to a glorious close.
"Remember," said Lord Kitchener, when bidding adieu to your Commander, "Remember, once you set foot upon the Gallipoli Peninsula you must fight the thing through to a finish".'

General Hamilton in his address to the troops about to assault the beaches.

15GW218 Horatio Herbert Kitchener, Secretary of State for War, appointed the overall commander and each British general to command the corps and divisions for the Gallipoli campaign.

15GW212 General Sir Ian Standish Monteith Hamilton, commander of the Mediterranean Expeditionary Force, was assigned the task of landing the invading force on Turkish territory.

15GW217 Australian troops embark for their assault on Gallipoli on 25 April, 1915.

'Officers and men – In conjunction with the Navy we are about to undertake one of the most difficult tasks any soldier can be called upon to perform, and a problem that has puzzled many soldiers for years past. That we will succeed I have no doubt, simply because I know your full determination to do so... We are going to have a real hard and tough time of it until... we have turned the enemy out of our first objective...'

Part of General Birdwood's address to the troops under his command about to assault the beaches.

'Expect heavy losses by bullets, by shells, by mines and by drowning.'

Hunter Weston in his address to the troops under his command about to assault the beaches.

15GW212 Lieutenant General William Riddell Birdwood, commanded the Australian and New Zealand Army Corps, which landed at what became known as Anzac Cove.

15GW214 Major General Sir Aylmer Hunter-Weston, commanded the British 29th Infantry Division.

15GW219 British and New Zealand troops leaving for the shores of Gallipoli 25 April, 1915.

1915

15GW220 Preparing a scramble net on board a British battleship for troops to disembark.

15GW144a The SS *River Clyde* troop transport before she had been modified by having sally-ports cut into her sides to land troops from gangways once she had been run aground close to the beach.

15GW221 Modifications being carried out on the SS *River Clyde*; machine gun positions and armour plate being fitted for the landing at Cape Helles.

15GW144 Fench troops of the vaunted Foreign Legion being taken to shore on a raft pulled by a steam tug.

15GW211 Troops disembarking on rowing boats.

15GW222 Scrambling aboard the rowing boats.

15GW144b A steam tug towing a raft containing French troops toward the shore at Gallipoli.

15GW223 Last minute kit inspection before these British soldiers leave their transport for the enemy shores.

15GW228 British troops disembarking by means of a minesweeper.
15GW226 British troops leaving the SS *Nile* to land on the beaches.

15GW225 Packed with British troops, a minesweeper heads for the beaches.

15GW230 British soldiers leaving the troop transports.

15GW229 Australian troops boarding minesweepers.

15GW234 Men of the Australian Artillery being landed at Gallipoli.

15GW241 Men crowd the rails of this transport, awaiting their turn to disembark.

15GW234 9th Battalion A.I.F. on board the destroyer HMS *Beagle*.

15GW235 Men of the 1st Battalion Border Regiment on board a minesweeper.

15GW231 Ships' lighters packed with men form up ready for the assault on the beaches.

15GW224 The British landing force under tow towards the beach.
15GW232 A tug boat pulls a raft bearing an artillery piece towards the beaches.

15GW237 Packed with troops, this vessel heads towards Turkish territory.

15GW288 Heading for the beach.

15GW265 Turkish troops had plenty of time to prepare for the landings.

15GW250 British troops landing from rowing boats.

15GW289 A Turkish counter-attack on one of the beaches as depicted in a German newspaper.

15GW290 Very full small boats landing troops on packed beaches.

15GW263 British troops making a fine target for the Turkish defenders.

15GW179 Turkish battery equipped with Krupp 77 mm field guns.

AUSTRALIAN & NEW ZEALAND ARMY CORPS
G.O.C: Lieutenant General Sir W. Birdwood

1st AUSTRALIAN DIVISION
Major General W. T. Bridges

1st Australian Brigade:
1st (New South Wales) Battalion
2nd (New South Wales) Batt
3rd (New South Wales) Batt
4th (New South Wales) Batt

2nd Australian Brigade:
5th (Victoria) Battalion
6th (Victoria) Batt
7th (Victoria) Batt
8th (Victoria) Batt

3rd Australian Brigade:
9th (Queensland) Battalion
10th (South Australia) Batt
11th (Western Australia) Batt
12th (Sth & Wtrn Australia & Tasmania) Ba

I (New South Wales) Field Artillery Brigade (1st, 2nd & 3rd Batteries)
II (Victoria) Field Artillery Brigade (4th, 5th & 6th Batteries)
III (Queensland) Field Artillery Brigade (7th, 8th & 9th Batteries)
1st, 2nd & 3rd Field Companies, Engineer

15GW268 Corps commander: Lieutenant General Sir W. Birdwood.

15GW267 General Sir Ian Standish Monteith Hamilton, commanding the Mediterranean Expeditionary Force for the invasion of Gallipoli.

15GW271

29th Division
Major General A. G. Hunter-Weston, CB

15GW269

86 Brigade
2/Royal Fusiliers
1/Lancashire Fusiliers
1/Royal Munster Fusiliers
1/Royal Dublin Fusiliers

87 Brigade
2/South Wales Borderers
1/King's Own Scottish Borderers
1/Royal Inniskilling Fusiliers
1/Border Regiment

88 Brigade
4/Worcestershire Regiment
2/Hampshire Regiment
1/Essex Regiment
1/5th Royal Scots (TF)

XV Brigade, Royal Horse Artillery (B, L & Y Batteries)
XVII Brigade, Royal Field Artillery (13th, 26th & 92nd Batteries)
CXLVII Brigade, Royal Field Artillery (10th, 97th & 368th Batteries)
460th (Howitzer) Battery, Royal Field Artillery
4th (Highland) Mountain Brigade, Royal Garrison Artillery (TF) (Argyllshire Battery and Ross Cromarty Battery)
90th Heavy Battery, Royal Garrison Artillery
14th Siege Battery, Royal Garrison Artillery
1/2nd London, 1/2nd Lowland & 1/1st W. Riding Field Companies, Royal Engineers (TF)
Divisional Cyclist Company

Royal Naval Division
Major General A. Paris, CB

1st (Naval) Brigade
Drake Battalion
Nelson Battalion
Deal Battalion, Royal Marine L I

2nd (Naval) Brigade
Howe Battalion
Hood Battalion
Anson Battalion

3rd (RM) Brigade
Chatham Battalion, Royal Marine L I
Portsmouth Battalion, Royal Marine L I
Plymouth Battalion, Royal Marine L I

Motor Maxim Squadron (Royal Naval Air Service)
1st & 2nd Field Companies, RN Divisional Engineers
Divisional Cyclist Company

Operation Order No 1 issued by Lieutenant Colonel Tizzard, 1st Battalian Munster Fusiliers 24 April 1915

1. Information
Information points to a landing on Turkish territory being opposed. The detail of landing of the covering force has already been issued

2 Intention?
The first objective is the village of Sed-Ell-Bahr (exclusive) and Forts 1 and 2 inclusive. This line will be attacked vigorously as soon as a landing has been effected.

3 Objectives?
Z coy will land on the starboard side of the vessel and attack the line from the village to half way between it and Fort 1. X coy will land on the port side and attack the line extending from half way between the village and fort 1 to fort 1. W coy will support Z coy. Y coy will support X coy?
Two m/c guns will follow X coy and select positions to assist attack.

As soon as the line allotted to the Battalion has been secured the Battalion will push on and effect a junction with the Dublin Fusiliers on the right and the Lancashire Fusiliers on the left
The plan being that half an hour after the towed boats had landed the River Clyde would run aground on V beach, troops would emerge through the sally ports on to gangways running along each side towards the bows of the vessel. These gangways then lead down to two barges, which form a gangway to shore.
The barges forming the gangway to shore will be towed alongside the vessel, and with the forward impetus, they would shoot forward when the vessel was beached. They could then be manoeuvred into position so that the troops could run along them to shore and so land quickly, form up, and develop the attack.

NEW ZEALAND & AUSTRALIAN DIVISION
Major General Sir A. Godley

New Zealand Brigade:
- Auckland Battalion
- Canterbury Batt
- Otago Batt
- Wellington Batt

4th Australian Brigade:
- 13th (New South Wales) Battalion
- 14th (Victoria) Batt
- 15th (Queensland & Tasmania) Batt
- 16th (South & Western Australia) Batt

New Zealand Field Artillery Brigade (1st, 2nd & 3td Batteries)
New Zealand Field Howitzer Battery
Field Company, New Zealand Engineers

ANZAC Corps Troops
7th Indian Mountain Artillery Brigade (21st [Kohat] Battery and 26th [Jacob's] Battery)
Ceylon Planters Rifle Corps

The *River Clyde* was carrying 2,000 soldiers, mostly from the 1st Battalion, Royal Munster Fusiliers and men from the 1st Battalion, Royal Dublin Fusiliers. There were also two companies of the 2nd Royal Hampshire from 88 Brigade.

For the assault on **V Beach** the units were positioned on SS *River Clyde* as follows :

1st Battalion, Royal Munster Fusiliers

Forward main deck holds
X Company (Captain G.W. Geddes)
Z Company (Captain C.L. Henderson)

Forward lower holds
Y Company (Major C.H.B. Jarret)
W Company (Major W.K. Hutchins)

After holds
Two companies of the 2nd Battalion Royal Hampshire Regiment.
One company of the 1st Battalion Royal Dublin Fusiliers

Also on board SS *River Clyde*
One company West Riding Field Engineers.
Two Sub-Divisions Field Ambulance.
One platoon Anson Battalion Royal Naval Division
One signal section.
A total of 8 machine guns.

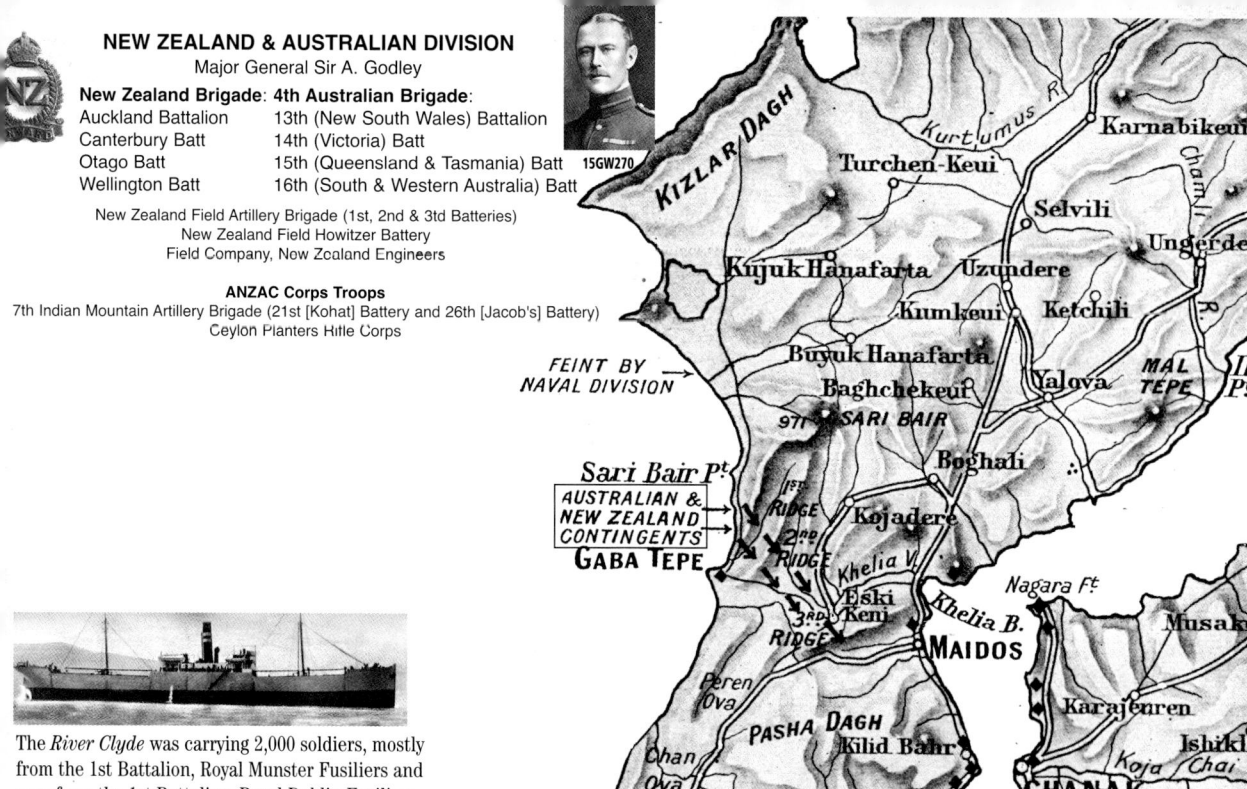

CORPS EXPÉDITIONNAIRE D'ORIENT
Commander: General d'Amade

1st DIVISION
General Masnou

Metropolitan Brigade: 175th Regiment Regiment de Marche d'Afrique
(2 Battalions Zouaves, 1 Battalion Foreign Legion)

Colonial Brigade: 4th Colonial Regiment (2 Battalions Senegalese, 1 Battalion Colonial)
6th Colonial Regiment (2 Battalions Senegalese, 1 Battalion Colonial)
6 Batteries of artillery (75-mm)
2 Batteries of artillery (65-mm)

1915

15GW253 SS *River Clyde*, with sally ports cut into the hull and with gang planks in position. Men were to run down these and onto boats, scrambling across them and then up the beach.

The SS *River Clyde* beached under the guns of the Turkish defenders and immediately became a death trap. Three attempts to land made by companies of Munsters, Dublins and Hampshires all ended in costly failure. Further landing attempts were abandoned and the surviving soldiers waited until nightfall before attempting to get on shore again.

Members of *River Clyde's* crew maintained a bridge of boats from the ship to the beach and recovered the wounded. For their bravery six of them were decorated with Victoria Crosses: Commander Unwin (aged 51); Midshipman George Drewry (aged 20) ; Midshipman Wilfred Malleson (aged 18); Able Seaman William Williams (aged 34); Seaman George Samson (aged 26) and Sub-Lieutenant Arthur Tisdall (aged(24) of the Royal Naval Division. Williams was killed in the landing and was decorated posthumously. Samson was severely wounded the next day but survived. On his return to Scotland he was handed a white feather while wearing civilian clothes. Tisdall was killed on 6 May 1915 with the 6th (Hood) Battalion RND in the Second Battle of Krithia.

15GW253 SS *River Clyde* after its beaching, showing sand-bagged positions for machine guns on the bow.

15GW251 A diaorama of the action depicting the landing of troops from the SS *River Clyde*.

15GW272 Commander Edward Unwin (aged 51).

15GW273 Midshipmen George Drewry (aged 20).

15GW274 Midshipmen Wilfred Malleson (aged 18).

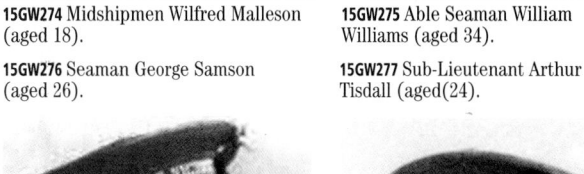

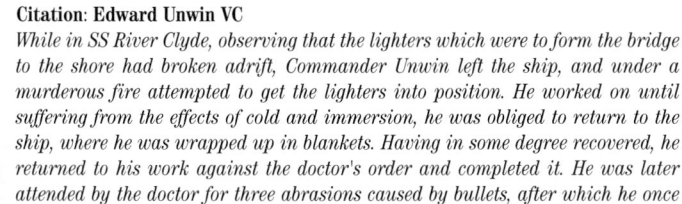

15GW275 Able Seaman William Williams (aged 34).

15GW276 Seaman George Samson (aged 26).

15GW277 Sub-Lieutenant Arthur Tisdall (aged 24).

Citation: Edward Unwin VC

While in SS River Clyde, observing that the lighters which were to form the bridge to the shore had broken adrift, Commander Unwin left the ship, and under a murderous fire attempted to get the lighters into position. He worked on until suffering from the effects of cold and immersion, he was obliged to return to the ship, where he was wrapped up in blankets. Having in some degree recovered, he returned to his work against the doctor's order and completed it. He was later attended by the doctor for three abrasions caused by bullets, after which he once more left the ship, this time in a lifeboat, to save some wounded men who were lying in shallow water near the beach. He continued at this heroic labour under continuous fire, until forced to stop through physical exhaustion.

Citation: Sub Lieutenant Tisdall VC

Hearing wounded men on the beach calling for assistance, jumped into the water, and, pushing a boat in front of him, went to their rescue. He was, however, obliged to obtain help, and took with him, on two trips, Ldg. Smn. Malia; and on other trips, Ch. P.O. Perring and Ldg. Smn. Curtis and Parkinson. In all, Sub. Lieut. Tisdall made four or five trips between the ship and the shore, and was thus responsible for rescuing several wounded men under heavy and accurate fire.

15GW252 An amazing photograph taken from the Vickers machine gun positions on the prow of the SS *River Clyde*. Men can be seen bunched up on the shore, attempting to take cover from the Turkish machine-gun fire and accurate sniping; the lighter directly in front is packed with dead and wounded. Men from the *Clyde* had been in the water positioning the boats and holding them together. Six of these men were later awarded the Victoria Cross for their actions.

Citation: Midshipman G. L. Drewry VC
He sssisted Commander Unwin at the work of securing the lighters under heavy rifle and maxim fire. He was wounded in the head, but continued his work and twice subsequently attempted to swim from lighter to lighter with a line.

Citation: Midshipman W. Malleson VC
Assisted Commander Unwin, and after Midshipman Drewry had failed from exhaustion to get a line from lighter to lighter, he swam with it himself and succeeded. The line subsequently broke, and he afterwards made two further but unsuccessful attempts at his self-imposed task.

Citation: Able Seaman W.C. Williams VC
He held on to a line in the water for over an hour under heavy fire, until killed.

Citation: Seaman G. Samson VC
He worked on a lighter all day under fire, attending wounded and getting out lines; he was eventually dangerously wounded by maxim fire.

Captain Guy Nightingale, who was on the *Clyde*, wrote:
The water was shallower than we thought and the Clyde *was stuck about 80 yards out – none of us felt it ground, there was no jar. As she beached two companies of the Dublins in 'Tows' came up on the Port side and were met with terrific rifle and machine-gun fire. They were literally slaughtered like rats in a trap. Many men sank owing to the weight of their equipment and were drowned. The carnage on V Beach was chilling, dead and wounded lay at the water's edge, which was tinted crimson from their blood. After being set adrift by their steam pinnaces, the boats had to row the last few hundred yards to the shore. The Turks waited until the men tossed their oars and were within 20 yards of the shore and then swept them with fire.*

I don't think that out of the 240 men in the boats more than 40 got ashore without being hit. Most were killed outright, many sank from exhaustion and loss of blood and were drowned, the water by this time was red with blood. As each boat got near the shore snipers shot down the oarsmen. The boats then began to drift, and machine-gun fire was turned onto them, you could see the men dropping everywhere, and of the first boat load of 40 men only 3 reached the shore, all wounded.

15GW278 Turkish Maxim machine guns were able to rake the SS *River Clyde* with fire and pin down the British on the beach.

15GW279 Turkish snipers picked off the British soldiers packed close together on the beach.

15GW233 Barbed wire defences awaited the invaders.

15GW236 Lancashire Fusiliers approaching the shores. At this point Turkish small arms fire was striking the men in the boats.

15GW264 Packed boats approaching the defended beaches.

15GW409 British troops assaulting Turkish positions.

15GW292 Landing at ANZAC cove.

15GW206 Reinforcements coming ashore.

15GW346 Australian and New Zealand troops make a leisurely landing at ANZAC cove, 25 April, 1915.

15GW291 Landing at ANZAC cove.

15GW293 Landing at ANZAC cove. At all the landing beaches the Allies had barely established a toehold on the Gallipoli Peninsular by the end of the day.

15GW294 View from the bridge of the *River Clyde* looking forward towards V Beach, now occupied and being transformed into a supply depot.

15GW297 The supplies dump under the wall of Sedd el Bahr fort.   **15GW298** The supplies dump alonside Sedd el Bahr fort, looking inland.

15GW299 Sedd el Bahr fort, with three gun emplacements wrecked by accurate shell fire from Royal Navy ships. French troops took over this area once the landings had been secured.

15GW295 With the beach area secured, the beached *River Clyde* acts as a bridge for lighters filled with supplies to moor alongside and unload their cargoes.

15GW296 A view from the vantage point of the prow of the *River Clyde* at the encampments, horse lines and dumps.

15GW300 British Army canvas packs, and other other equipment from the 533 dead and wounded who landed at W Beach.

15GW301 Captain Willis VC.  **15GW302** Major Bromley VC.  **15GW303** Sergeant Richards VC.  **15GW304** Sergeant Stubbs VC.

15GW307 'Six VCs Before Breakfast' painting of the action at W Beach.

15GW304 Corporal Grimshaw VC.  **15GW304** L/Corporal Keneally VC.

1915
94

15GW287 French troops occupying the ground around Fort Seddul Bahr.

15GW313 The Allies were ashore but only just; here French troops man their front line trench not far inland from Fort Seddul Bahr.

15GW308 Shaded areas showing the limited penetration of Turkish soil the Allies were managing to hold.

15GW314 Turkish reinforcements arrive to contain the landing and hopefully drive the invaders back into the sea.

15GW316 The Turkish infantryman.

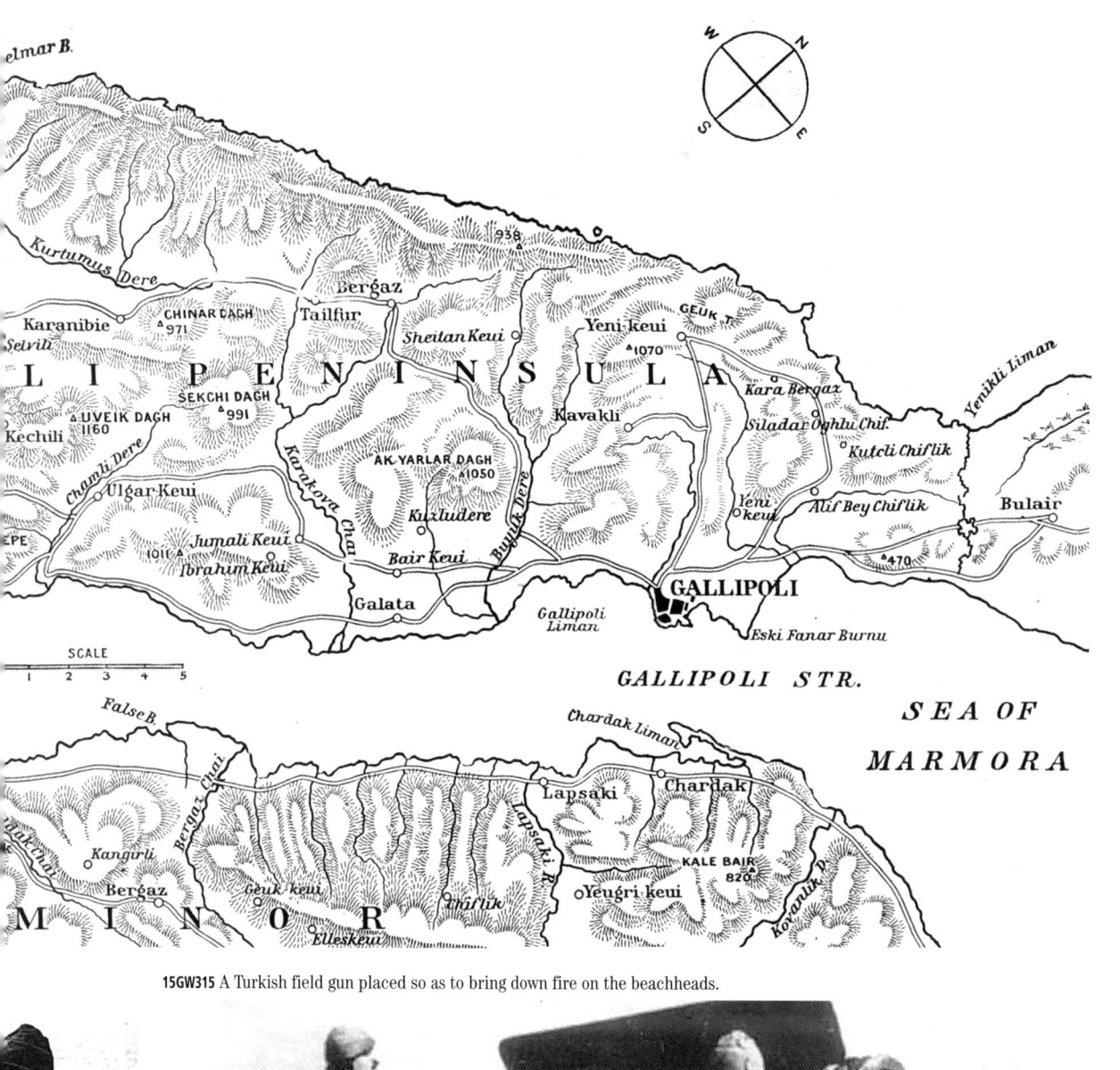

15GW315 A Turkish field gun placed so as to bring down fire on the beachheads.

15GW330 A French 75mm field gun crew firing towards the hill, Achi Baba, a vantage point behind the Turkish lines.
15GW333 A big gun in a Turkish fort blown from its carriage by an explosion from a ship's 15-inch guns.

15GW336 French troops occupying V Beach, with the *River Clyde* in the background.

15GW331 French troops in a ruined fort observing shell explosions on the Turkish strongpoint of Achi Baba.

15GW334 Obsolete Turkish guns wrecked during the bombardment by allied warships.

15GW335 Horses watering beneath the walls of Sedd el Bahr fort.

15GW337 The *River Clyde*, with a landing pontoon in the foreground.

15GW332 British Royal Engineers pile-driving timbers to extend a landing jetty.

15GW329 Royal Engineers extend a landing jetty, pile-driving timbers into the seabed

15GW339 British troops making primitive bombs from empty food tins.

15GW338 Turkish rifles and ammunition captured by the British.

15GW340 Officer Commanding the British 29th Division, Major General AG Hunter-Weston, at Army Corps HQ.

15GW342 Rear Admiral Stuart Nicholson making his way along a communication trench after visiting a Naval Observation Station at Cape Helles.

15GW323 Anzacs, shortly after landing, crowd the beach awaiting orders to advance inland.

15GW343 Australian infantry preparing to move from the beach area in the Dardanelles.

15GW344 'Colonial troops in their dug-outs' is how the original caption describes these Anzacs.

15GW348 The beach, now renamed Anzac Cove, soon became congested with Australian and New Zealand infantry.

15GW347 Anzac Cove looking towards the headland of Ariburnu (north). Little Ariburnu, known as Hell Spit, is to the south of the cove.

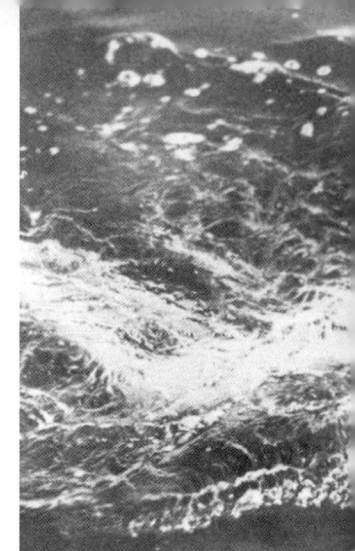

15GW351 Despite Turkish shells continually exploded in and around Anzac Cove, this did not deter soldiers from bathing in the sea.

15GW356 Lieutenant General Birdwood outside his HQ at Anzac Cove.

15GW349 Men of the 1st Australian Light Horse Regiment taking over new dugouts.

15GW350 Australian infantry stage a bayonet charge for the camera. Note the grins on some of the faces of the attackers.

15GW354 Lieutenant General Birdwood, commander of the Anzac Corps joins his men in a morning swim.

15GW355 A bonus from the shelling – fish killed by explosions in the water provides a welcome addition to their army diet for these soldiers.

15GW352 An Australian sniping team at a forward trench: officer has taken over the rifle; soldier is using the officer's binoculars and the sniper's observer is using a trench periscope to locate any unwary Turk who might expose his head over the trench parapet.

15GW362 Demonstrating a Japanese trench mortar mounted on an improvised stand.

15GW359 Australian infantry in captured Turkish trenches at a position named Lone Pine, August 1915.

15GW360 Looking back over the ground from Lone Pine, with Australian unburied corpses.

15GW357 An 18-pounder light field gun firing on Turkish postions at Anzac Cove.
15GW361 A captured trench at Lone Pine with both Turkish and Australian dead on the parapet. The body with the white armband is an Australian.

15GW358 15GW317 15GW318 Turkish troops awaiting another attack against their defensive positions.

15GW345 Turkish troops digging trenches as they prepare to defend their homeland.

15GW374 When heavy Royal Artillery guns were brought ashore the British proceeded to pound the Turkish defenses in earnest. A 60-pounder battery in action.
15GW373 Charge! Yet another gallant attempt to dislodge 'Johnnie' Turk from his well concealed postitions.

15GW375 A British soldier teasing Turkish snipers.

15GW385 In a captured Turkish position, British soldiers grab a rest.

15GW376 A British Vickers machine gun team using a contraption to fire the gun without sticking their heads above the parapet.

15GW377 Turks launching an attack to try and drive the Allies into the sea. The Turks mounted a massive attack on 18 May 1915, using 42,000 troops, but they were repulsed, suffering 10,000 casualties.

15GW378 British officers question four captured Turkish soldiers as the two guards look on.

15GW401 Turkish soldiers under a flag of truce meeting Australians in No Man's Land to bury the dead.

15GW405 Australians and British troops digging graves in No Man's Land.

15GW402 A Turkish officer is led blindfolded into the Allied lines to negotiate a temporary cease-fire so that the large numbers of putrefying corpses lying out in No Man's Land can be buried.

15GW403 Over 2,000 Turks and fallen Anzacs were buried during the truce, which lasted from 7.30 am to 4.30 pm on 24 May 1915.

15GW400 Turks turned up with their rifles, so the Australians removed the bolts until the job was finished.

15GW404 Disarmed Turkish soldiers begin the task of burying their fallen comrades.

15GW406 Before they were buried the identity disc had to be found on the corpse and a note made.

15GW478 Turkish troops who fell on the scrub covered slopes of Chocolate Hill resisting a British attack from Suvla Bay.

15GW455 A drink of water for a captured Turkish prisoner.

15GW479 A Turkish sniper under guard by his Australian captors.

15GW480 The Australian camp at Anzac Cove, with living quarters crammed together close to the shore. Boxes of supplies can be seen piled up close to the water's edge.

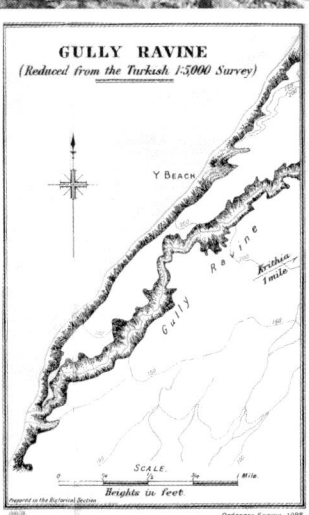

15GW379 The entrance to Gully Ravine photographed in September 1915.

Gully Ravine is a deep natural cut through the land on the western side of the Gallipoli peninsula running from the foothills of Achi Baba to the sea. Achi Baba should have been captured soon after the landings, 27 April 1915, but the village was never taken by the invading forces. Gully Ravine is over thirty metres deep in places and afforded shelter in which the British army was able to set up dressing stations, stables, supply dumps and rest areas situated along the numerous smaller gullies branching off from it.

15GW408 Bathers on Gully Beach, September 1915.

15GW410 The road leading up from the beach and into Gully Ravine, May 1915.

15GW420 British shelters in Gully Ravine.

15GW417 Officers' shelters overlooking Gully Beach.

15GW411 Bringing supplies by mule up Gully Ravine, following heavy rain.

15GW416 A British army horse drawn ambulance struggling through Gully Ravine, after heavy rain had turn the rough track into a stream bed.

15GW413 Royal Fusiliers carrying up supplies through Gully Ravine.

15GW240 Human debris – bodies lying among the wire at the top of Gully Ravine.

15GW418 The seriously wounded being taken by mule-drawn ambulance down Gully Ravine to an awaiting ship.

15GW415 Walking wounded British soldiers making their way to Gully Beach for transfer to a ship.

15GW414 Turkish captives being taken down Gully Ravine following a failed attack.

15GW193 Turkish captives awaiting shipment to Egypt.

15GW353 Wounded and prisoners being loaded onto boats to take them out to waiting ships.

15GW419 Six horses were needed to pull this ambulance through the deep mud of Gully Ravine.
15GW386 Stretcher bearers bringing in wounded to a British army aid post.

The Battle for Gallipoli had very quickly reached stalemate. The landing at Suvla Bay, which commenced on the night of 6 August 1915, was intended to support a breakout from the Anzac sector, five miles to the south and get the offensive moving once more.

Initial opposition to the landing at Suvla Bay was light, however, the British commanders mishandled it from the outset. The situation very quickly reaching the same impass that prevailed on the Anzac and Helles fronts. On 15 August, after a week of indecision and inactivity, the British commander at Suvla, Lieutenant General Sir Frederick Stopford, was dismissed.

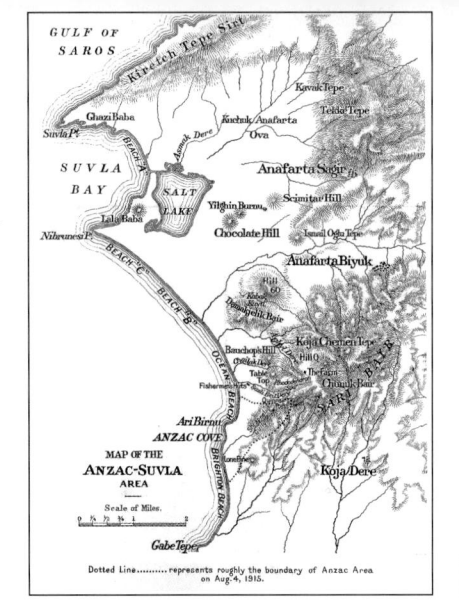

15GW422 Lieutenant General Sir Frederick Stopford commanded the Suvla operation.

15GW425 Anzac soldiers, having landed on the beach at Suvla Bay, await orders to move in land.

15GW48 Lighters were turned into fresh water containers and again back into transports when the time came to withdraw from Suvla Bay.

15GW426 Once the Turkish defenders had responded in strength to the fresh invasion the beaches were targeted.

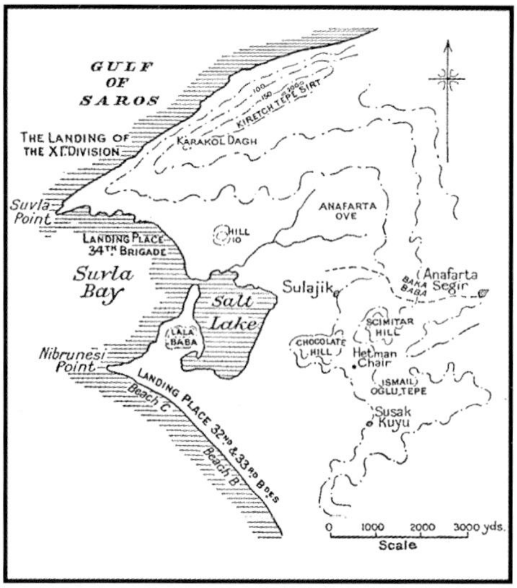

15GW423 Lighters packed with troops head for the landings at Suvla Bay.

15GW424 Soldiers form up and march off inland at Suvla Bay.

15GW427 As at the other invasion beaches, the ones at Suvla soon became clogged with Allied troops.

15GW431 British troops camped on the edge of the beach at Suvla Bay.

15GW433 British troops filling their water bottles at a canvas reservoir.

15GW435 British soldier reading a paper on the front line trench fire step.

15GW437 Australian stretcher bearers bringing a casualty into an aid station.

15GW434 British wounded waiting for their turn to be evacuated from B Beach.

15GW432 British troops taking up a water bowser at Suvla Bay.

15GW441 Constructing trench periscopes and rifle frames for sniping over the trench fire step.

15GW421 Using a trench periscope in the front line.

15GW430 Stretcher cases being taken off the beach to waiting transports.

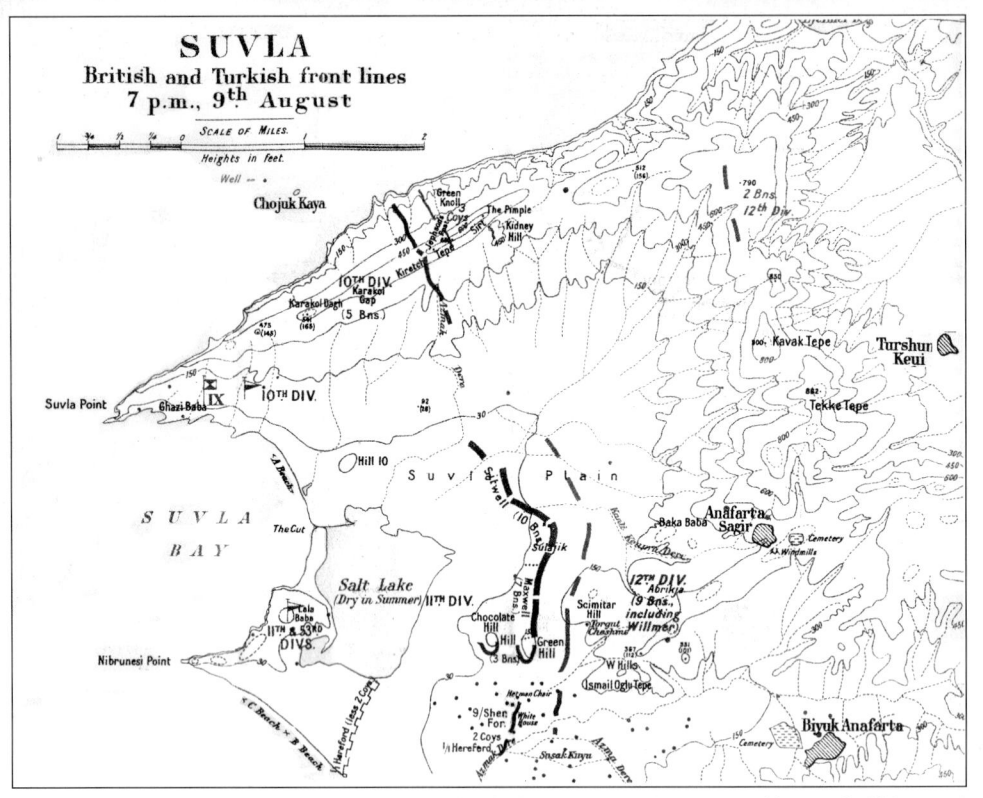

SUVLA
British and Turkish front lines
7 p.m., 9th August

The Allies were barely off the beach and soon the Turkish defenders were occupying strong positions on the high ground.

15GW442 With the Turkish forces commanding the heights, the Allies were firmly stuck.

15GW449 Major General Frederick Hammersley, commanding 11th (Northern) Division, was relieved of his command.

15GW444 British soldiers in dugouts.

15GW448 Yeomanry in the fire trench

15GW487 Sandringham House, Royal residence in Norfolk, at the turn of the twentieth century. It was the favoured residence of King George V.

In 1908 King Edward VII asked his land agent at Sandringham, Francis Beck, to form a company of soldiers for the 5th Battalion Norfolk Regiment. Beck recruited more than 100 part-time soldiers to form E Company in this Territorial battalion. All the men belonged to the staff of the royal estate. Members of the gentry, such as Francis Beck and his two nephews became the officers; the estate's foremen, butlers, head gamekeepers and head gardeners were the NCOs; the farm labourers, grooms and household servants made up the rank and file.

During E Company's first action on the afternoon of 12 August, 1915, at Suvla Bay, Gallipoli, every man simply disappeared during an attack on Turkish positions. No bodies were found and no men turned up as prisoners of war. The British Commander-in-Chief in Gallipoli, Sir Ian Hamilton, appeared as puzzled as everyone else. He reported:

'There happened a very mysterious thing, the Norfolks had drawn somewhat ahead of the rest of the British line; the ground became more wooded and broken but Colonel Beauchamp with sixteen officers and 250 men, still kept pushing on, driving the enemy before him. Among these ardent souls was part of a fine company enlisted from the King's Sandringham estates. Nothing more was ever seen or heard of any of them. They charged into the forest and were lost to sight and sound. Not one of them ever came back.'

Even King George V could gain no further information other than that the Sandringhams had conducted themselves with 'ardour and dash'. (Later, in 1919, burial places were found.)

15GW488 King George V.

15GW489 Captain Francis Beck.

15GW490 Officers of the 1/5th Battalion, Norfolk Regiment, before leaving for Gallipoli. The two ringed officers were nephews of Captain Beck, officers in E Company (Sandringham Estate men). The officer commanding the battalion was Colonel Sir Horace Beauchamp, who came out of retirement.

15GW489 Norfolk Regiment cap badge.

Some of these officers were among those who simply disappeared when they surged ahead of the other battalions during an attack by 163 Brigade.

1915
132

15GW486 Queen Alexandra Caroline Marie Charlotte Louise Julia. Alexandra was the mother of the reigning monarch, George V, and was queen mother. She was styled 'Her Majesty Queen Alexandra'.

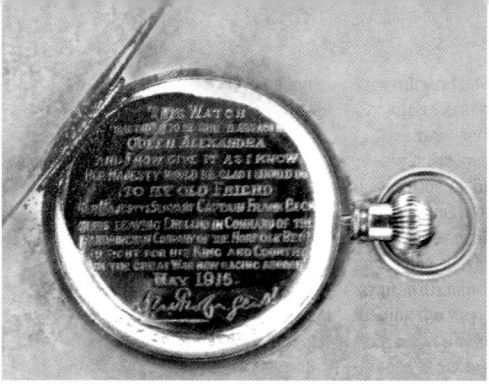

Before the Sandringham Company left England Queen Alexandra presented Captain Frank (Francis) Beck with a gold watch engraved as follows:

THIS WATCH WAS PREPARED AND ENGRAVED FOR
QUEEN ALEXANDRA
AND I NOW GIVE IT AS I KNOW HER MAJESTY WOULD BE
GLAD I SHOULD TO MY OLD FRIEND
HIS MAJESTY'S SERVANT CAPTAIN FRANK BECK
ON HIS LEAVING ENGLAND IN COMMAND OF THE
SANDRINGHAM COMPANY OF THE NORFOLK REGT
TO FIGHT FOR HIS KING AND COUNTRY
IN THE GREAT WAR NOW RAGING ABROAD. MAY 1915

After the war came news from Turkey of a gold fob-watch, looted from the body of a British officer in Gallipoli. It was Frank Beck's. The watch was later presented to Margeretta Beck, Frank's daughter, on her wedding day.

15GW492 British infantry attacking Turkish positions at Anzac on 8 August. When the Norfolks attacked four days later they vanished and it remained a mystery as to what happened to them until September 1919. The Graves Registration Unit reported finding 180 graves scattered over an area of a square mile, 800 yards behind the Turkish front line. They simply stated 'We have found the 5th Norfolks'. Only two were identified, Privates Barnaby and Cotter.

1915
133

15GW443 Royal Irish Fusiliers.

15GW446 15GW447 15GW445 British dead scattered about and near the lines; and the impossibility of burying them led to almost unbearable smells.

15GW396 Lord Kitchener, along with Lieutenant General Birdwood, completes his inspection. The new Commander-in-Chief, General Monro, had recommended evacuation of the Gallipoli Peninsula: Kitchener concurred.

15GW438 A substantial harbour was established at Suvla Bay, which would help facilitate evacuation of troops.

15GW396 Lord Kitchener arrived at Gallipoli to check the situation for himself. He is seen here with Lieutenant General Birdwood.

15GW436 A despatch rider braves the snipers' bullets as he makes the perilous coast road journey between Anzac Cove and Suvla Bay.

15GW341 General Sir Ian Hamilton talking to Major General Ellison on the morning of his departure for England, 17 October 1915, after being relieved of his command for the total failure of the Gallipoli landings, which had resulted in the deaths of over 130,000 on both sides.

15GW450 General Sir Charles Monro replaced Hamilton as Commander-in-Chief of the Mediterranean Expeditionary Force.

15GW451 Army chaplains of the Church of England, Roman Catholic and Presbyterian Churches attend this multiple burial.

15GW457 Tommies say goodbye to their fallen comrades that they are leaving behind.

15GW382 British troops on Gully Beach awaiting evacuation. Turkish shells are exploding in the sea and these men seem unperturbed.

15GW389 Abandoned British positions.

15GW391 A device for fooling the Turks: a cocked rifle is positioned in the abandoned Allied trenches with a water timing mechanism for triggering the weapon.

15GW395 The evacuation underway.

15GW452 Troops embarking.

15GW453 Leaving Gallipoli.

15GW454 Three of the very last Turkish prisoners to be taken from Gallipoli during the Allied withdrawal.

15GW390 A squad of stuffed 'reinforcements' ready to be taken to man the trenches.

15GW392 Preparations for evacuation underway at Anzac Cove.

15GW394 Indian troops loading supplies for evacuation at Anzac Cove.

15GW388 HMS *Cornwallis*, the last ship to leave Gallipoli in the evacuation of 19-20 December 1915.
15GW387 Stores at Suvla Bay, set alight to prevent their use by the Turks.

15GW429 Turkish officers, after having successfully defended their homeland, watch the allied ships withdrawing from the Gallipoli peninsula.

15GW610 Winston Churchill resigned as First Lord of the Admiralty following the disastrous Gallipoli Campaign.

Information used in this chapter was based on the following titles in the **Battleground Europe** series of guide books:
Gallipoli by Nigel Steel; *Gallipoli – Gully Ravine*, *Gallipoli – Anzac Landing*, *Gallipoli – Suvla August Offensive*, *Gallipoli – Anzac Sari Bair*, *Walking Gallipoli* by Stephen Chambers; *Gallipoli – Landings at Helles* by Huw & Jill Rodge.
These are available from Pen & Sword History Books Ltd.

Chapter Three: The Battle of Neuve Chapelle

15GW482 Indian troops preparing to attack at Neuve Chapelle.

15GW493 British infantry sheltering from the winter weather.

The small village of Neuve Chapelle, situated twenty miles south of Ypres, was where the British launched their first major attack from the static trench lines that stretched across Belgium and France. It was undertaken by the British First Army under the command of Sir Douglas Haig. The purpose of the attack was to capture the German trenches in and around the village and move on to capture the high ground of Aubers Ridge.

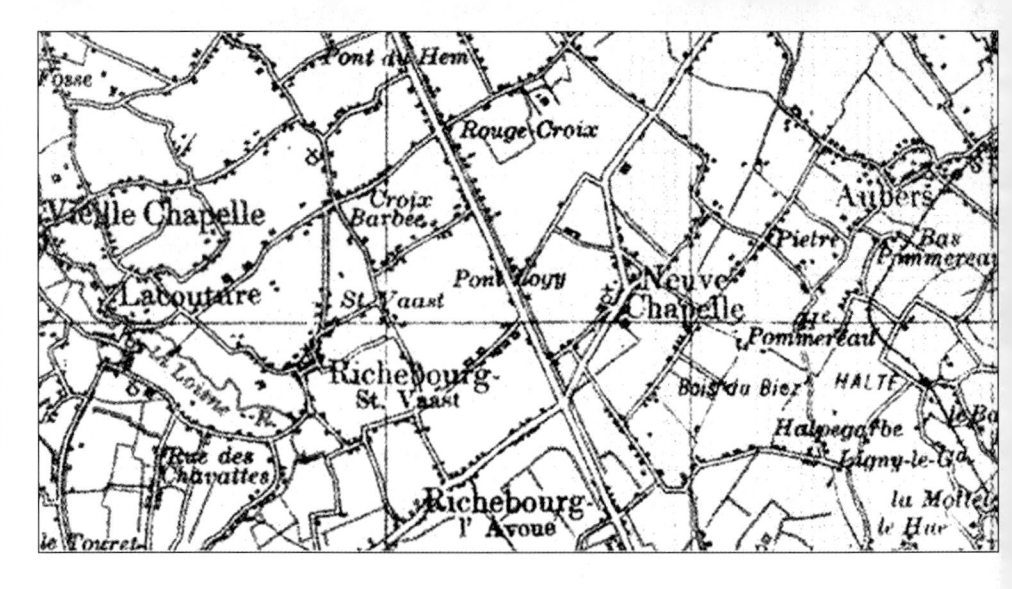

15GW504 Dehra Dun Brigade, Headquarters Section, Brigade Signals in the field at St Floris, France. The men are posing carrying out signalling duties: operating field telephones, a Morse key, the use of bicycle equipped battalion runners. Also, on the grass, can be seen signalling flags.

5GW483 Indian soldiers constructing trenches with sandbags and placing barbed wire at the front. Over 1.5 million Indian soldiers fought as volunteers for Great Britain in the First World War.

15GW509 Indian troops charging at Neuve Chapelle, March 1915.

15GW511 The Rajah of Rutlam with his father, Sir Pertab Singh, and one of the general's aides.

15GW512 Sir Pertab Singh, reads a popular English magazine with his son, the Rajah of Rutlam, seated beside him.

15GW513 Sir Pertab Singh with Allied officers, French and British, in France.

15GW515 Sir Douglas Haig introducing Lieutenant General Sir Pertab Singh to French General Joffre.

15GW514 Sir Douglas Haig and Lieutenant General Sir Pertab Singh.

15GW510 A painting of Sir Pertab Singh leading the Jodhpur Lancers through a French village.

15GW505, 15GW507, 15GW506, 15GW508
Gurkha troops of the Indian Corps training before the forthcoming attack on German positions on the Western Front.

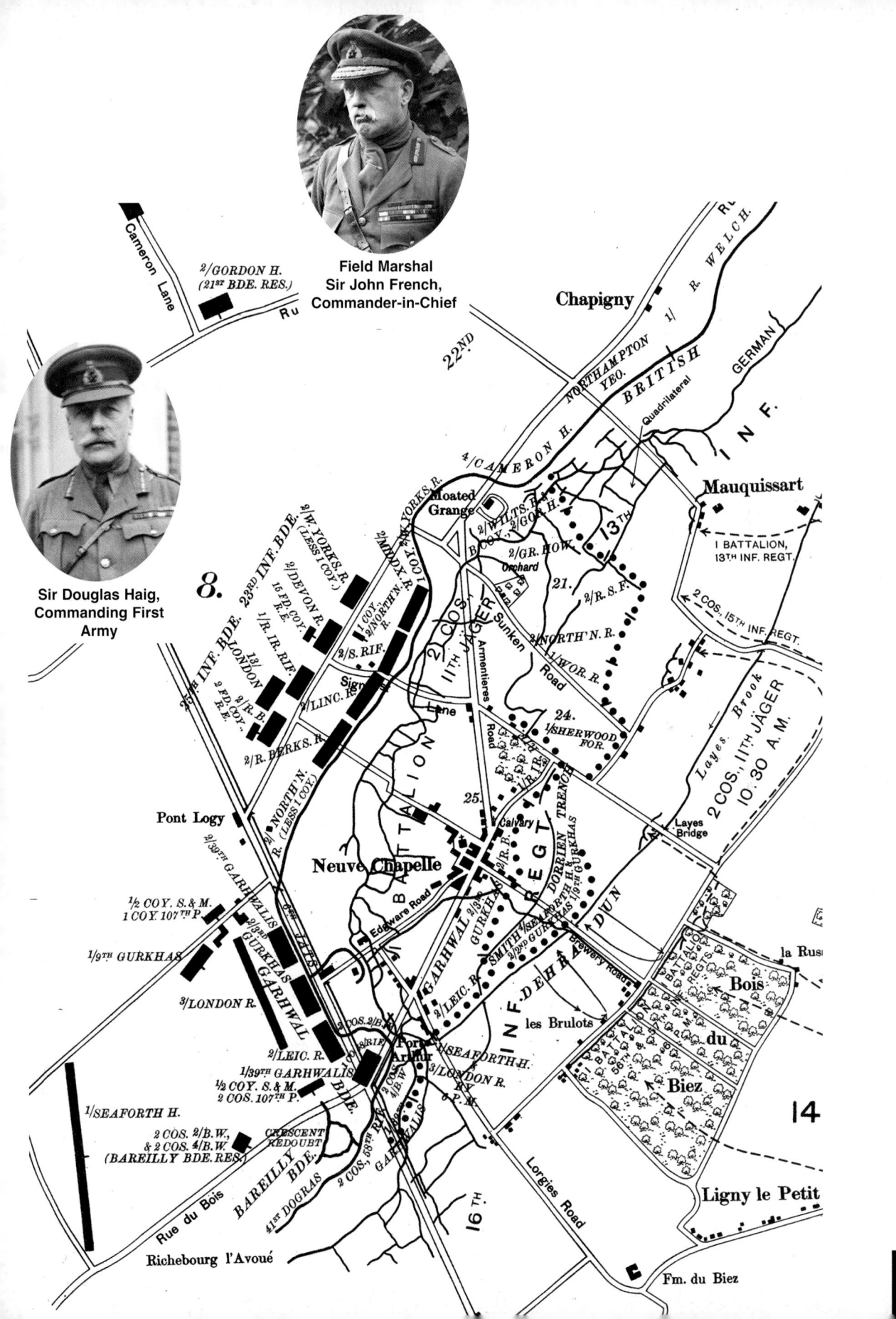

Field Marshal Sir John French, Commander-in-Chief

Sir Douglas Haig, Commanding First Army

1915
151

Sir Henry Rawlinson
General Officer Commanding IV Corps

7th Infantry Division

General Officer Commanding:
Major General Sir Thompson Capper

20 Brigade
GOC: Brigadier General F. Heyworth

- 1/Grenadier Guards 
- 2/Scots Guards 
- 2/Border Rgt
- 2/Gordon Highldrs
- 6/Gordon Highldrs (TF)

21 Brigade
GOC: Brigadier General H. Watts 

- 2/Bedfordshire Rgt 
- 2/Yorkshire Rgt 
- 2/Royal Scots Fus 
- 2/Wiltshire Rgt

22 Brigade
GOC: Brigadier General S. Lawford 

- 2/Royal West Surrey Rgt
- 2/Royal Warwickshire 
- 1/Royal Welsh Fus 
- 1/Sth Staffordshire 
- 8/Royal Scots (TF)

Divisional Artillery:
XXXVIII (H.) Artillery Brigade:
67, 31st (H.), 35th (H.) Batteries

Brigade Ammunition Columns: 68
XIV R.H.A. B.A.C. XXII B.A.C. XXXV B.A.C. XXXVII (H.)
Divisional Ammunition Column 7th D.A.C.

Engineers:
54th, 95th, 69 & 2/Highland
Signals Service:
70 Divisional Signals Company
Medical Unit:
7th Field Ambulance
21st, 22nd, & 23rd Mobile Veterinary Sections
Divisional Train: 7th

8th Infantry Division

General Officer Commanding:
Major General Sir Francis Davies

23 Brigade
GOC: Brigadier General R. Pinney

- 2/Devonshire Rgt 
- 2/West Yorkshire Rgt 
- 2/Cameronians Rifles 
- 2/Middlesex Rgt

24 Brigade
GOC: Brigadier General F. Carter 

- 1/Worcestershire Rgt 
- 2/East Lancashire Rgt 
- 1/Sherwood Foresters 
- 2/Northamptonshire Rgt
- 4/Cameron Highldrs (TF)

25 Brigade
GOC: Brigadier General A. Lowry Cole 

- 2/Lincolnshire Rgt 
- 2/Royal Berkshire Rgt 
- 1/Royal Irish Rifles 
- 2/Rifle Brigade 
- 13/London Rgt (TF)

Divisional Mounted Troops:
C Sqn. 1/Northumberland Hussars
76 8th Cyclist Company
Divisional Artillery:
V Brigade, Royal Field Artillery (RFA)
O Battery, Z Battery
XXXIII Artillery Brigade:
32nd, 33rd, 36th Batteries
XLV Artillery Brigade:
1st, 3rd, 5th Batteries
CXXVIII (H.) Artillery Brigade
77th, 55th (H.), 57th (H.) Batteries
Brigade Ammunition Columns:
78 V RHA B.A.C.; XXXIII B.A.C.; XLV B.A.C.;
CXXVIII (H.) B.A.C.
Divisional Ammunition Columns: 8th D.A.C.

Engineers:
2nd, 15th, 1/1/Home Counties Companies
Divisional Signals Companies
Pioneers
Medical Units:
8th, 24th, 25th Field Ambulances:
Mobile Veterinary:
15th Divisional Train

1915
152

Sir James Willcocks
General Officer Commanding Indian Corps

Meerut Division

General Officer Commanding:
Lieutenant General Sir C.A. Anderson

Dehra Dun Brigade 
GOC:
Brigadier General C.W. Jacob

Bareilly Brigade
GOC:
Brigadier General W.M. Southey

1 Bn Seaforth H   1/4 Bn Seaforth H   6 Bn Jat L Inf   2 Bn Gurkha Rifles   9 Bn Gurkha Rifles

Garwhal Brigade 
GOC:
Brigadier General G.C. Blackader

2 Bn Black Watch   1/4 Bn Black Watch   41 Bn Dogra Regt   58 Bn Vaughan's Rifles   125 Bn Napier's Rifles

2 Bn Leicestershire Rgt   1/3 Bn London Rgt   39 Bn Garhwal Rifles   3 Bn Gurkha Rifles   8 Bn Gurkha Rifles

Divisional Mounted Troops:
4th Cavalry
Divisional Artillery:
IV Brigade, Royal Field Artillery (RFA)
14th & 66th Batteries, IV Brigade Ammunition Column
IX Brigade, RFA
20th & 28th Batteries, IX Brigade Ammunition Column
XIII Brigade, RFA
8th & 44th Batteries, XIII Brigade Ammunition Column
110th Heavy Battery, Royal Garrison Artillery
30th Battery of XLIII (Howitzer Brigade) RA
Heavy Battery Ammunition Column
Meerut Divisional Ammunition Column

Engineers:
3rd & 4th Companies, 1st King George's Own Sappers and Miners
Signals Service:
Meerut Signal Company
Divisional Pioneers:
107th Pioneers
Supply & Transport:
Meerut Divisional train
Medical Units:
19th & 20th British Field Ambulances
128th, 129th and 130th Indian Field Ambulances

Lahore Division

General Officer Commanding:
Lieutenant General Sir H. D. Keary

Ferozepore Brigade 
GOC:
Brigadier General R. Egerton

Sirhind Brigade
GOC:
Brigadier General W. Walker VC

3n Connaught Rangers   9th Bhopal Inf   57th Wilde's Rifles   129th Baluchis   4/London Regt

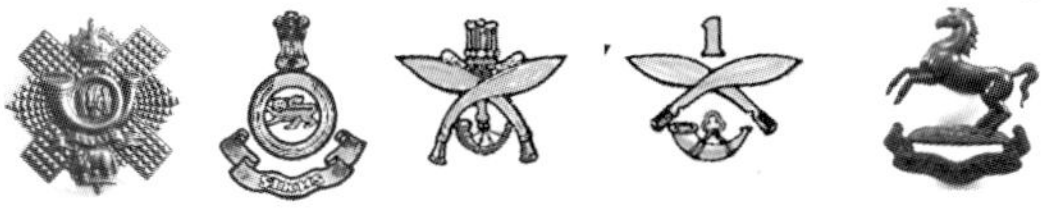

Jullundur Brigade 
GOC:
Brigadier General E. Strickland

1/Highland LI   15th Sikhs   1/1st Gurkhas   1/4th Gurkhas   4/Liverpool Regt

1/Manchester Regt   47th Sikhs   59th Scinde Rifles   4/Suffolk Regt

Divisional Mounted Troops:
15th Lancers (Cureton's Multanis)
Divisional Artillery:
V Brigade, Royal Field Artillery (RFA)
64th, 73rd & 81st Batteries, V Brigade Ammunition Column
XI Brigade, RFA
83rd, 84th & 85th Batteries, XI Brigade Ammunition Column
XVIII Brigade, RFA
59th, 93rd & 94th Batteries, XVIII Brigade Ammunition Column
109th Heavy Battery, Royal Garrison Artillery (4.7-inch guns)
XLIII (Howitzer Bde, RA (40th & 57th Batteries)
Heavy Battery Ammunition Column
Lahore Divisional Ammunition Column

Engineers:
20th & 21st Companies, 3rd Sappers and Miners
Signals Service:
Lahore Signal Company
Pioneers:
34th Sikh Pioneers
Supply & Transport:
Lahore Divisional train
Medical Units:
7th & 8th British Field Ambulances
111th, 112th and 113th Indian Field Ambulances

1915

15GW521 British and Indian officers of the 57th Wildes Rifles, Ferozepore Brigade.

15GW519 Men of A Coy, 2 Battalion, Black Watch, share a trench with Indian troops.

15GW538 Men resting at 21 Brigade's headquarters shortly before the attack on Neuve Chapelle.

15GW537 Moving up heavy artillery at Neuve Chapelle prior to the attack in March.

15GW541 British guns at Neuve Chapelle firing on the German positions.

15GW543 British infantry pass the time with a game of cards as they wait in reserve trenches during the attack on 10 March, 1915.

15GW542 Indian troops manning a French Benet-Mercie, 1909, Hotchkiss light machine gun.

15GW545 Wire entanglements laid by the Germans in front of the village of Neuve Chapelle.

15GW517 An unsure German grenadier seeks to locate his unit's position near Tahure, January 1915.

1915

15GW540 German infantry at Neuve Chapelle prior to the attack in March 1915.

15GW546 Reserve troops resting during a march from Armentières to Neuve Chapelle.

15GW547 German soldiers in Neuve Chapelle shortly before the March fighting.

15GW549 German position inside the village of Neuve Chapelle.

15GW550 German work detail repairing defences and mending roads.
5GW544 Some of the German defenders of Neuve Chapelle before the British attack.

15GW551 2/Royal Scots Fusiliers advancing at Neuve Chapelle.

15GW530 Bodies of men of the 2/Scottish Rifles killed on the first morning of the attack

15GW553 Among the ruined houses in the village of Neuve Chapelle.

15GW552 British dead from the first wave of the attack at Neuve Chapelle.

15GW556 Neuve Chapelle was devastated by the bombardments.

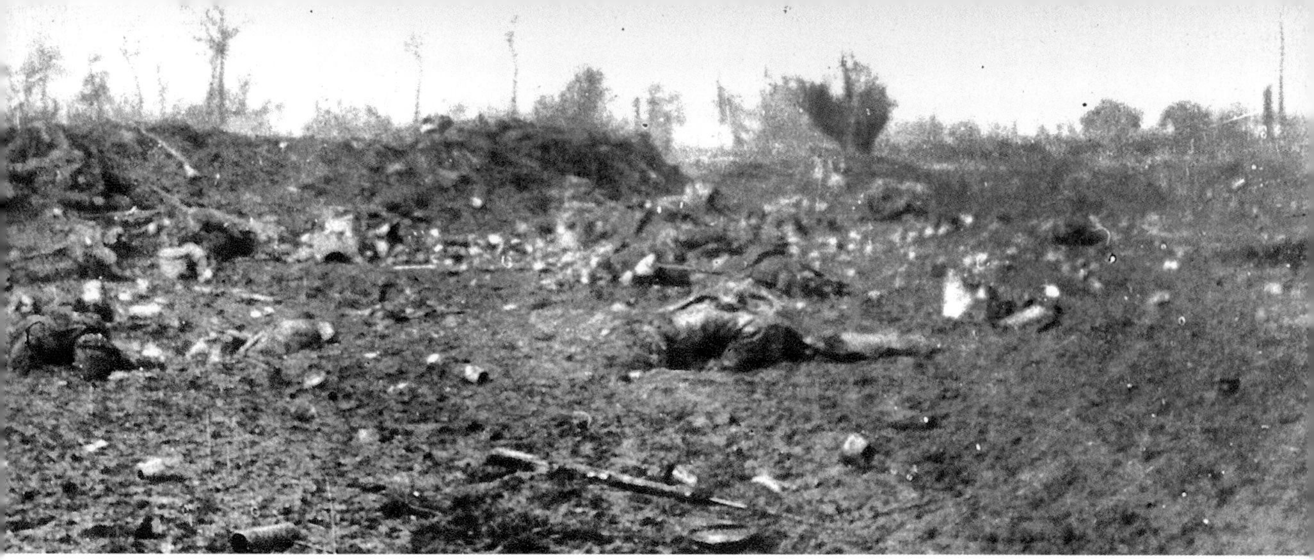

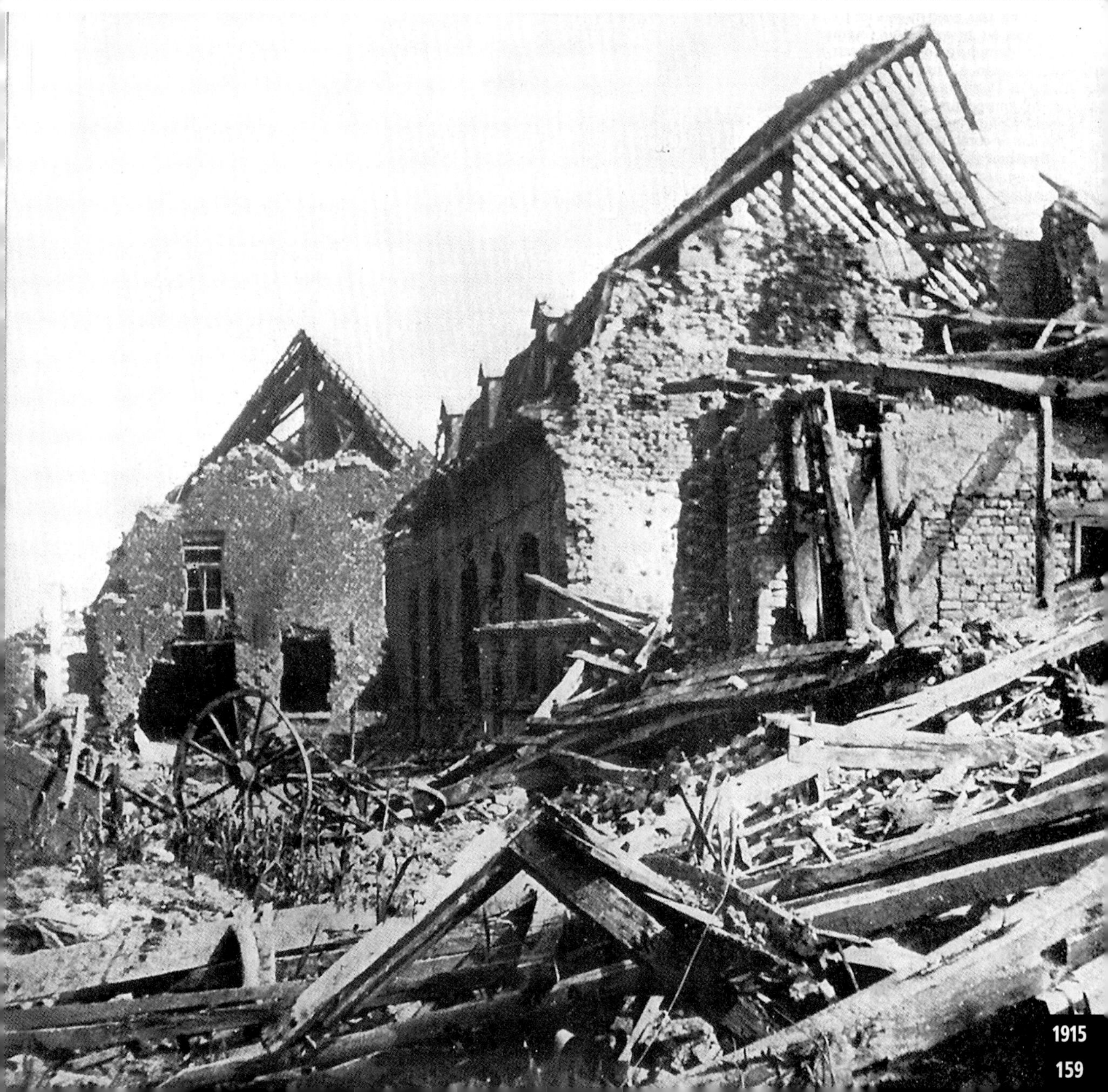

15GW494 Germans surrendering to men of the Worcestershire Regiment during the fighting for Neuve Chapelle.

15GW498 German prisoners having their pockets turned out following their capture during the fighting for Neuve Chapelle.

15GW497 British gunners cut down by German machine guns in the village of Neuve Chapelle. The dead are still waiting to be cleared away after the fighting.

15GW495 Minutes after their capture in their trenches, these German soldiers stand with their hands raised.

Lieutenant Colonel E. C. F. Wodehouse, commanding officer of the 1st Battalion the Worcestershire Regiment, was among the nine officers killed leading the attack.

15GW501 British dead lying among the barbed wire near Neuve Chapelle.

1915

15GW557 The main street of Neuve Chapelle.

15GW496 Men of the 1st Battalion Worcestershire Regiment the captured village of Neuve Chapelle guarding prisoners

15GW559 A British soldier in the ruins of village of Neuve Chapelle.

15GW558 A German machine gun post with armour plated shield in the captured village.

15GW565 A lone survivor in Neuve Chapelle.

15GW563 Captured German positions in Neuve Chapelle.

15GW568 An artist's depiction of the battlefield of Neuve Chapelle with the wood – Bois de Biez – on the right.

15GW560 A vertical positioned camera fitted so as to photograph the trenches, used for the first time at the Battle of Neuve Chapelle.

15GW561 A victim of 'friendly fire', this aircraft had been flying low observing the attack on 10 March 1915 when a British shell enroute towards the enemy lines struck it, knocking it from the sky. Both pilot and observer were killed.

15GW502 British wounded in the German trenches near Neuve Chapelle.

15GW554 German trenches in the woods near Neuve Chapelle.

15GW555 German soldiers in positions behind the lines.

15GW562 German prisoners of war captured at the Battle of Neuve Chapelle parading through an English street.

15GW566 A woman at the roadside shakes her fist at these German prisoners captured at Neuve Chapelle, on their way to a camp near Aldershot.

Information used in this chapter was based on the following title in the **Battleground Europe** series of guide books:
La Bassée – Neuve Chapelle by Geoffrey Bridger.
This is available from Pen & Sword History Books Ltd.

Chapter Four: The Second Battle of Ypres – Hill 60 – Gas

15GW620 British infantry attacking.

15GW616 British troops prepare for a gas attack.

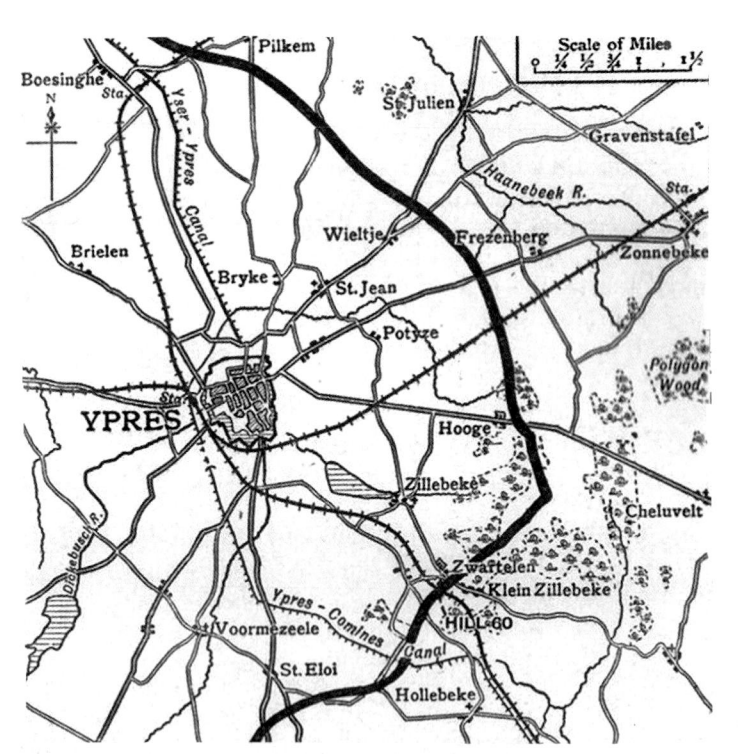

Belgian, British and French commanders were determined to deny the town of Ypres to the Germans but it left them in a difficult defensive position. The Allied forces found themselves defending a saucer-shaped salient of some fifteen square miles. Ypres was to the rear of the Allies' defensive front line in the centre of the saucer. The German Army, however, was in good defensive positions on the slightly higher ground around the rim of the saucer.

The Second Battle of Ypres was fought from 21 April – 25 May 1915 for control of the strategic Flemish town which stood in the way of the German Army reaching the Channel coast. By the end of the battle the Ypres Salient had been compressed and Ypres itself was closer to the front line. Bombardment gradually reduced the town to rubble. Poison gas had been used on the Eastern Front by the Germans but it still surprised the Allies in the west and about 7,000 gas casualties were admitted to field ambulances and casualty clearing station. From May to June, 350 British deaths were recorded from gas poisoning.

North of the Salient the Belgian army held the line of the River Yser, whilst the north end of the salient was held by two French divisions. The eastern part of the Salient was defended by one Canadian division and two British divisions.

15GW700 Ypres town square, with the Cloth Hall (*Lakenhalle*) and St Martin's Cathedral largely destroyed by shell fire.

15GW702, 15GW703, 15GW704 The Cloth Hall (*Lakenhalle*) Ypres in 1915.

1915

15GW705, 15GW706 The entrance to Ypres through the Menin Gate; in fact the gate had been removed some years before the war.

15GW701 Ypres, its destruction underway.

15GW617 Ypres' ramparts with added fortifications, occupied by British troops in 1915.

15GW618 Steady destruction underway at the Menin Gate area, Ypres.

15GW624 A former London bus lies wrecked, having brought up British troops from Ypres to just behind the Front.

15GW632 Men of the Honourable Artillery Company cleaning their rifles in a trench opposite the Mound at St Eloi (at the southern end of the Salient), April 1915.

15GW629 A senior officer entering his headquarters receives a salute. He is probably of general rank.

15GW627 Using outbuildings to snipe at the enemy positions. In the Salient buildings such as these would be flattened as the fighting continued over the years.

15GW626 A sniper in a stable waiting for a target.

15GW637 The Walker Periscope sniping attachment.

1915
174

15GW708 Men of a Territorial battalion, 1/5 York and Lancaster Regiment, soon after their arrival at the northern end of the Ypres Salient, are engaged in constructing a shelter, using a culvert which they have boarded over.

15GW707 A view from inside the culvert shelter looking out. The 1/5th Battalion York and Lancs have acquired a mixture of rifles: the Long Lee Enfield, usually associated with Territorial battalions, and the Short Lee Enfield.

15GW623 British high command trenches: where the water table was high with sides constructed trenches from sandbags well above ground.

15GW636 Honourable Artillery Company (HAC) officers in Sanctuary Wood, June 1915.

15GW634 Dugouts in Maple Copse in the Summer of 1915.

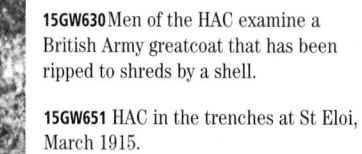

15GW628 A contraption for firing over the top of a trench. The Walker Periscope attachment consisted of an extra butt and a trigger pulling lever.

15GW630 Men of the HAC examine a British Army greatcoat that has been ripped to shreds by a shell.

15GW651 HAC in the trenches at St Eloi, March 1915.

15GW635 Dugouts in Sanctuary Wood August 1915.

1915
177

15GW638 Looking across No Man's Land at the German held village of Zillebeke. The German Front Line can be seen as a line of sandbags
15GW621 Germans occupying a barn, which serves as a lookout post, in Belgium.

15GW622 Germans have turned this farm building into a strongpoint.

15GW595 Germans in an elaborately constructed fire trench.

15GW621 Germans manning a front line trench.

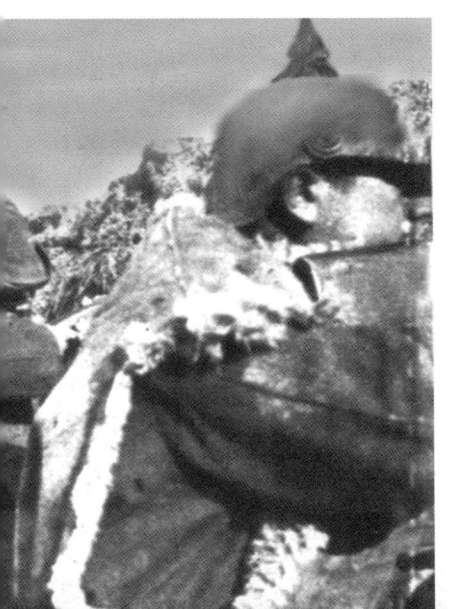

15GW601 Officers of the German General Staff with the Commander in Chief, Kaiser Wilhelm II.

15GW608 Soldiers pose with British bombs from an aircraft brought down behind the German lines.

15GW602 A German 77 mm field gun, on an improvised and precarious looking timber mount, positioned to fire at allied aircraft

15GW609 A French bomb, which failed to explode, dropped on German positions.

15GW610 A Roman Catholic priest and a Lutheran pastor unite to conduct a service for German troops. There could be little doubt left in the minds of the listeners as to which side the Almighty was favouring in this great war.

15GW596 Constructing trenches using multi-toned sandbags to aid camouflage effect. Note the wire netting used to hold the walls in place and the wooden implements for patting the sandbags into angular shapes – evidence of German efficiency.

15GW585 A German cavalry regiment pauses during the move north to join the advance guard to German operations around Ypres.

15GW586 At the end of a sap dug towards the Allied lines this Maxim machine gun team plan an unpleasant surprise for any would-be attackers.

15GW639 A German cyclist with a folding bicycle.

15GW632a Comforts of home – a German soldier repairing a greatcoat which bears the cuff title 'Gibraltar'. This was worn by three Hanoverian regiments that served in the British Army and garrisoned Gibraltar during the US War of Independence.

1915

15GW754 Earliest known photograph of Hitler in uniform.

15GW755 Hitler with his arms around two of his comrades; he is the one in the light coloured fatigue coat.

15GW756 Hitler, wearing a *pickelhaube*, in a headquarters dugout, where he served as a runner.

15GW752 Hitler's military identity discs: Bavarian Reserve Infantry Regiment 13, 3. Companie, Number 718.

15GW573 Bavarian Reserve Infantry Regiment 16, 1. Companie, Number 148.

15GW756 Taking no part in this fun band – all have make-shift instruments – Hitler stands, hands in pockets, looking on at this 'Band of Noise' rehearsal.

1915
185

15GW760 Hitler is seated right, with moustache.

15GW761 Hitler is seated left, with moustache.

15GW762 Again Hitler is seated on the outer edge of this group, front row, next to the officers.

15GW773 In 1915 Hitler was stationed in the French village of Fournes-en-Weppes, near Fromelles. He had already had a vicious 'blooding' in the First Battle of Ypres, after which he was promoted to corporal, decorated with the Iron Cross and served as a regimental runner.

1915
187

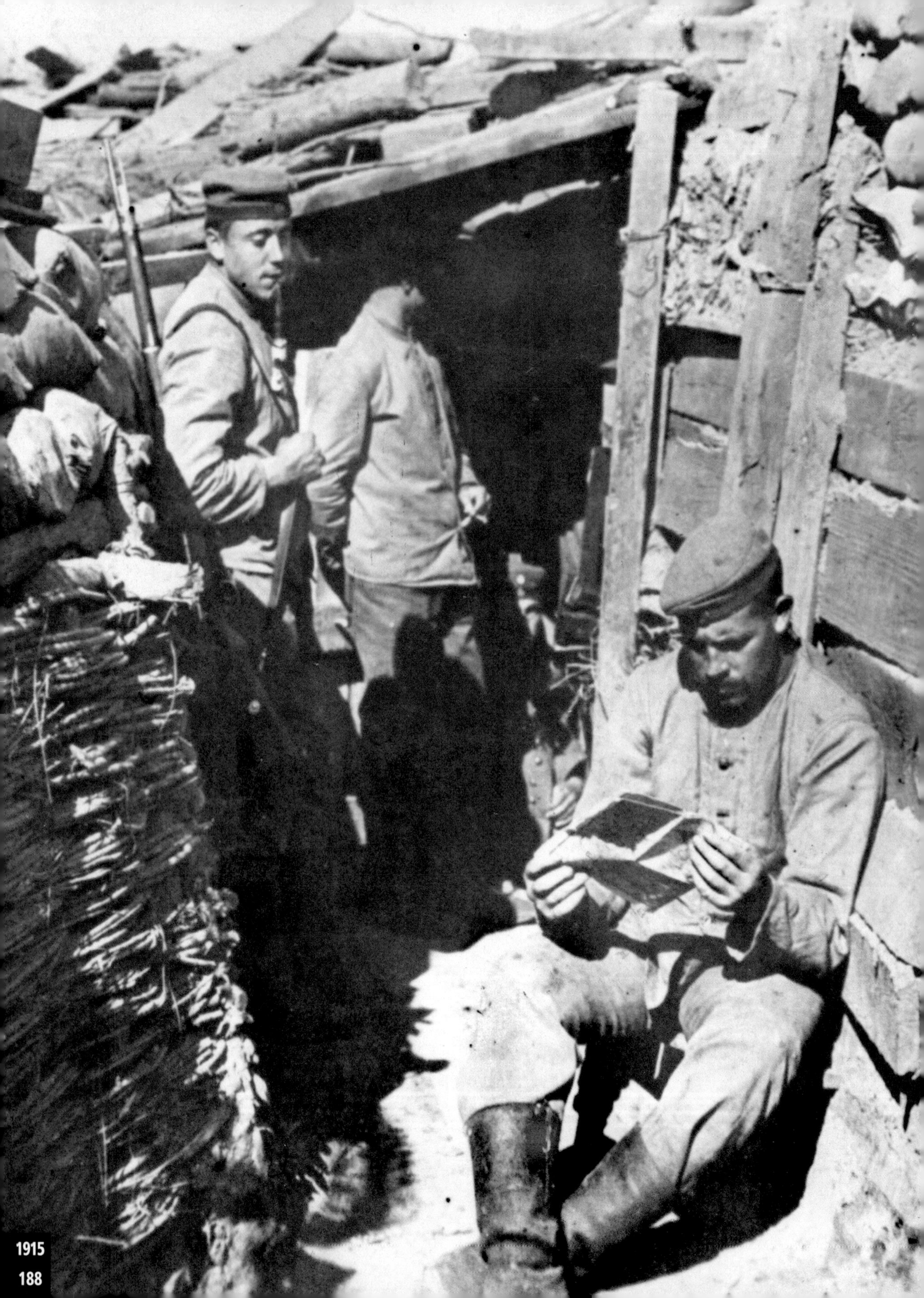

15GW593, 15GW594 Germans of the 127th Infantry Regiment (9th Württemberg) Infantry comfortably positioned on Hill 60. The trench sign reads 'Zug=Grenze' which could be loosely translated as 'Platoon Boundary'.

15GW763 Cramped quarters in this German trench (officer seated).   **15GW764** An officer emerging from his dugout.

15GW766 Germans attacking across a deep defensive trench covered with barbed wire.

15GW765 German troops constructing a railway behind the front.

15GW767 German casualties after an attack.

15GW589 Panoramic view of Hill 60 from the Allied second line, looking across the railway cutting towards the German positions, which may be discerned from the line of sandbags on the hillside.

15GW588 Looking across No Man's Land towards the German-held village of Zwarteleen; to the right of the village is a good view of the spoil heap formed when the Ypres–Comines railway was constructed and which, because of its height above sea level and surrounding land, was designated Hill 60 in 1914.

The Great War Illustrated in Colour
by Jon Wilkinson

15co01 After three monthsl in Egypt, these men were among Australians troops transported to the Greek island of Lemnos in March 1915, in preparation for the invasion of Gallipoli.

15co02 No specialized landing craft were designed for the invasion of Gallipoli – troops were landed by ships' boats and consequently much pre-invasion training was concerned with scrambling down rope netting wearing full equipment and carrying a rifle.

15co03 How the landing north of Gaba Tepe would have appeared. This is a reconstruction of the landings which were made at dawn on Sunday 25 April, 1915.

15co04 Putting on a spirited bayonet charge for the camera man; a staged action image, but it conveys the kind of mass attacks employed in attempts to overthrow the Turkish defences.

1915
4

15co06 Australian sniper using a wooden frame to hold a rifle and view through the sights of the weapon by means of two angled mirrors.

15co07 Viewing 'Johnnie Turk' through a trench periscope; the spotter would relay the direction of a target and the sniper would take a snap shot in the direction indicated.

15co11 Turkish gun crew overseen by a German artillery officer loading and firing a German gun – the 105 mm Feldhaubitz 98/09 howitzer.

15co08 A German propaganda postcard depicting a highly dramatized opposition to the Allied landings at Gallipoli. *The Dardanelles theatre of war: First Landings of English and French troops at Gallipoli.*

15co10 British troops attacking Turkish positions.

15co13 A view of V Beach and the established Allied landings at Seddul Bahr from the vantage point of the prow of the *River Clyde*: densly packed supply dumps can be seen crammed into every available space.

15co12 Turkish reinforcements resting during the march to oppose the landings.

15co15 A battery of British 60-pounder Mk I guns in action at Cape Helles in June 1915.

15col14 Royal Fusiliers carrying up supplies through Gully Ravine.

15GW378 British officers question four captured Turkish soldiers as their two guards look on.

15col09 A British soldier tempting Turkish snipers to give away their positions while others snatch some shut-eye.

15col20 A 210 mm heavy howitzer Mörser 10.

15col18 Men of A Company, 1/5th Battalion, York and Lancaster Regiment, based at Rotherham Drill Hall before the war, in trenches for the first time at Fleurbaix, on the southern edge of the wet Flanders plain.

15col19 Captain Hugh Parry-Smith, officer commanding C Company, 1/5th Battalion, York and Lancaster Regiment, based pre war at Birdwell Drill Hall, Barnsley, using a folding periscope (originally designed for looking over the top of crowds – such as at horse race meetings).

1915
13

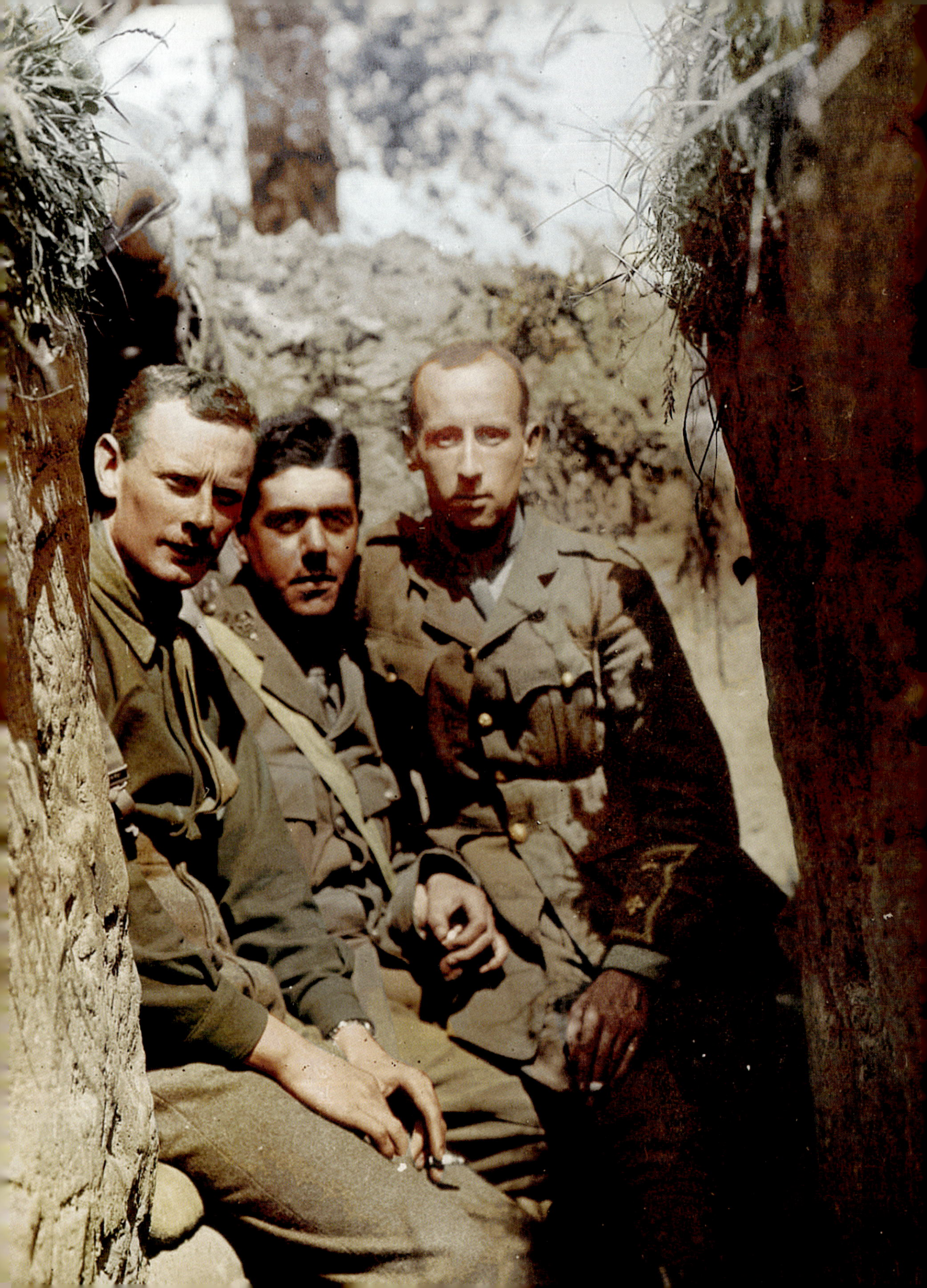

15col29 Three officers of the 1/5th Battalion, York and Lancaster Regiment. Captain George Hewitt invites fellow officers into his dugout on the Yser Canal. Left to right: Captain Hewitt, Lieutenant Cattle and Lieutenant Colver (the owner of the camera and photographic recorder of the battalion up until his death in December 1915).

15col28 Captain Hewitt, Lieutenant Cattle and Lieutenant Colver at the entrance to Hewitt's dugout on the banks of the Yser Canal, July 1915.

15col27 Captain Hewitt and Lieutenant Colver at the entrance to Hewitt's dugout.

Two days after this photograph was taken George Hewitt was shot in the head and wounded by a German sniper. He wrote of the incident:
'...it was the last place I would have expected to get hit. I was just on my way to have some food in my dugout, when suddenly I saw millions of stars and found myself on my knees clawing air... I bled like a pig.'
After a period of convalescence at home, he returned to the 2/5th Battalion and was killed in November 1917 at the Battle of Cambrai.

1915

1915
16

15col23 A British machine gun team in position in the Ypres Salient. The men are stripping down and cleaning their Vickers machine gun.

15col22 Men of a Highland battalion in a state of readiness in a trench on the Western Front.

1915

15col24 The British 18-pounder gun – a standard artillery piece during the First World War.

15col25 A Zeppelin over a British town on the East Coast – a version by a German artist.

15col26 A Zeppelin under attack by a RFC fighter – Digital reconstuction by Jon Wilkinson.

1915
22

15col30 Two Fokker *Eindecker* in combat with two Vickers F.B.5s with one of F.B.5s going down in flames. One of the crew, the operator of the front Lewis gun, has been depicted as choosing to leap to his death rather than burn (parachutes were not made available).
– Digital reconstruction by Jon Wilkinson.

15col31 An early dogfight between a Fokker *Eindecker* and a Vickers F.B.5 – Digital reconstruction by Jon Wilkinson.

15col21 (Over the page) Prior to the Battle of Loos, British infantry prime handgrenades for the attack –
a photograph coloured by Jon Wilkinson.

1915
24

15GW625 Photographed shortly after Hill 60 was captured on 16 April by men of the Royal West Kents, seen here consolidating their position.

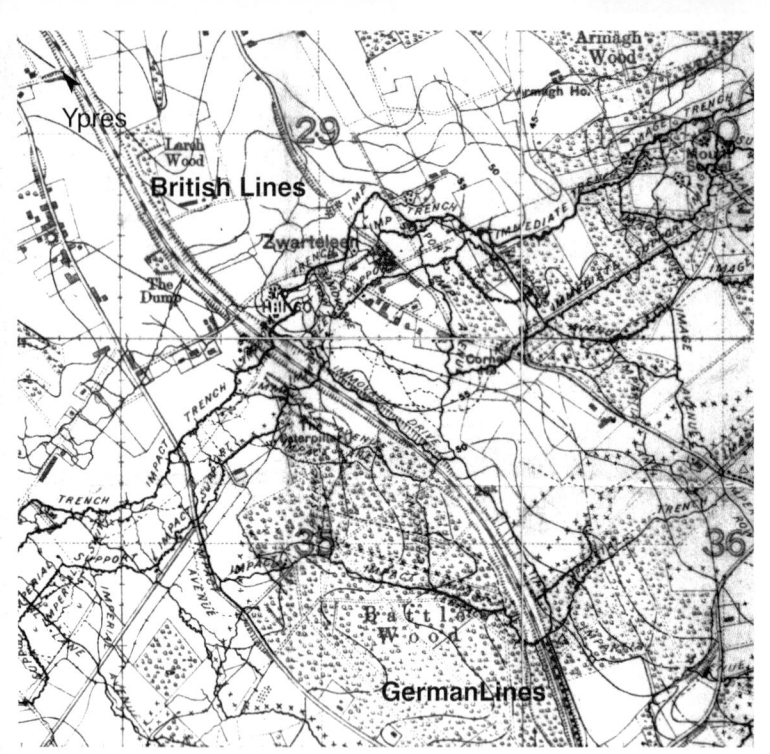

15GW592 The Bluff, a hard fought over area to the south of Hill 60.

15GW619 British Tommies enjoying a meal together out of the line

15GW646 Men of the 1/5th Battalion King's Own Royal (Lancasters) Regiment in trenches in the Ypres Salient.

15GW642 A Scottish battalion at Hill 60 in 1915.

15GW644 British troops at Hill 60 in 1915.

15GW643 British troops at Hill 60 in 1915.

15GW640 British soldiers at Hill 60 spot an aeroplane.

15GW641 A captain of at Scottish regiment armed with a telescope.

15GW779a 'Short back and sides – sir?' A break from the Front Line for necessary tidying up.

1915
197

15GW582 An artist's depiction of the new terror weapon being used for the first time against the French in the Ypres Salient, 22 April 1915. According to one observer, who noted white puffs of smoke that seemed to act as a signal:

'Almost at once a thick curtain of yellow smoke arose and was blown gently towards the French trenches by the north-east wind. This curtain, which advanced like the yellow wind of Northern China, offered the peculiarity that it spread thickly on the ground, rising to a height of some feet. Some of the French got clear in time, but many stood their ground and were overcome by the fumes dying poisoned. The fumes, rolled on over two kilometeres of ground from front to rear.'

15GW570 Germans laying out pipes for the poison gas.

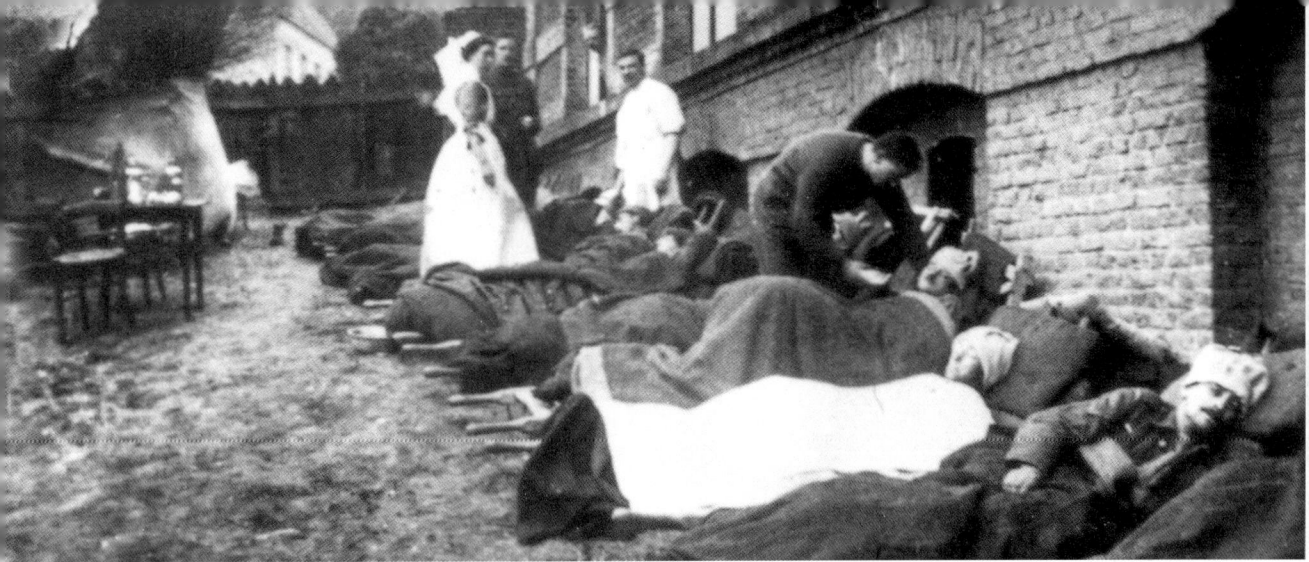

15GW614 British gas casualties from the fighting at Hill 60 recovering out in the open at No.8 Casualty Clearing Station, Bailleul.

15GW573 British wounded demonstrate for the camera the makeshift masks they adopted at Hill 60.

15GW615 Men of the 1st Battalion Cameronians seen here using a Vermorel liquid sprayer, containing a solution to disperse chlorine gas.

15GW647 British Tommies putting on a show for the camera to prove that they are not downhearted by the latest German methods to kill them.

1915

15GW569 The bodies of gassed French Morrocan troops near Langemark, 22 April 1915.

A series of photographs that appeared in the German press showing the capture of Hill 60:

15GW603 German medics giving first aid to wounde in a captured British position on Hill 60.

15GW604 British prisoners captured at Hill 60.

15GW605 The body of a dead British soldier in a trench captured by the Germans.

15GW606 A captured trench showing a pump for draining water and some dead British soldiers.

15GW578 A picture that appeared in a German newspaper in the Spring of 1915 showing German field ambulance orderlies treating a fellow soldier with oxygen, having suffered injury from asphyxiating gas. The caption read: 'Protective measures against British gas shells'. Clearly a propaganda ploy by the Germans to justify their introduction of the banned weapon. It would be late September of 1915, at the Battle of Loos, before the British used gas in retaliation.

Chlorine gas was the first killing asphyxiating agent used by the Germans in the war. By April 1915 the German Army had 168 tons of chlorine deployed in the Ypres Salient. In the first release of poisonous gas on the Western Front French Colonial troops from Martinique were targetted. At about 5 pm, the gas was released, forming a grey-green cloud that drifted into the trenches causing the terrified soldiers to retreat before it. A massive four and a half mile gap was broken open in the Allied line. However this opportunity for a break-through was not exploited as the German infantry were reluctant to follow through. French and Canadians reformed the line.

During the Second Battle of Ypres gas was used by the Germans on three more occasions: in April against the 1st Canadian Division; in May against the British at Mouse Trap Farm; and at Hill 60. In August chlorine gas was used on the Eastern Front against the Russians.

15GW571 Poisonous fumes seen rolling towards Russian positions on the eastern front. The photograph was taken by a Russian pilot in 1915.

15GW611 Pads of cotton waste were issued to British troops in May 1915, one month after the Germans first used poison gas in Flanders. Soda water was used to moisten the pads and, if not available, then urine was used as a readily available substitute.

15GW600 German officers equipped with gas masks and helmets. Each man has a signalling pistol for firing as well as Model 24 *Stielhandgranate* (handgrenades).

15GW572 A French soldier wearing the new steel helmet, 'Adriane', along with an early gas protection mask.

15GW575a, 15GW575b A complicated anti-poison gas system with an oxygen bottle, designed by the French and called the 'Masque Vanquit'. Note the horn to warn others of gas.

15GW574 Early French mask, named the 'Masque Robert', was made of India-rubber.

15GW581 A French Marine equipped with an early respirator, one of the more successful types being tested.

15GW648 Another French variation.

15GW579 'What a man at the Front looks like now' is the caption under this photograph of a soldier in the Honorable Artillery Company. Also added are the words 'The war-time holiday of the H.A.C. I have just got my new "respy" and I really look more of a nut than ever.'

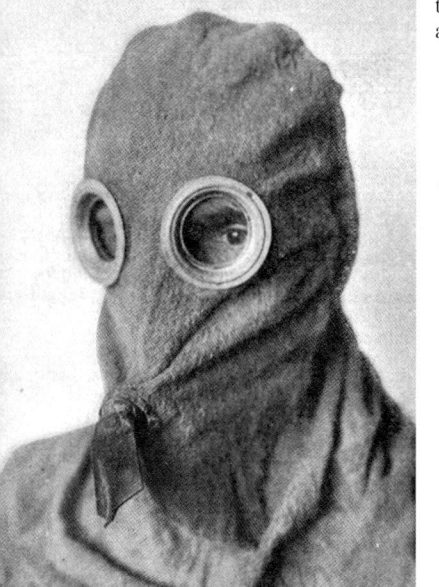

15GW580 Another attempt at anti-gas protection: this Highlander wears a mask, goggles and what appears to be a hood and gauze.

15GW649 An early British development.

15GW650 This German medical orderly carries breathing aids for the treatment of chlorine gas victims.

15GW577 Respirator parade for British soldiers: This regular drill was made necessary by the use of asphyxiating gas by the Germans.

15GW584 A British soldier with his dog at the entrance to a dugout near St Julien in the Ypres Salient. He is wearing a make-shift gas mask on his cap, which can be pulled down quickly over his face in the event of a poison gas attack.

15GW633 More developed equipment for this sniping team – a range-finding scope for the man spotting and a telescopic sight for the sniper.

15GW665 A sniper's position showing three hits on 'Huns', dated June 3 1915.

15GW666 British sniper wearing a grass-style camouflaged hood.

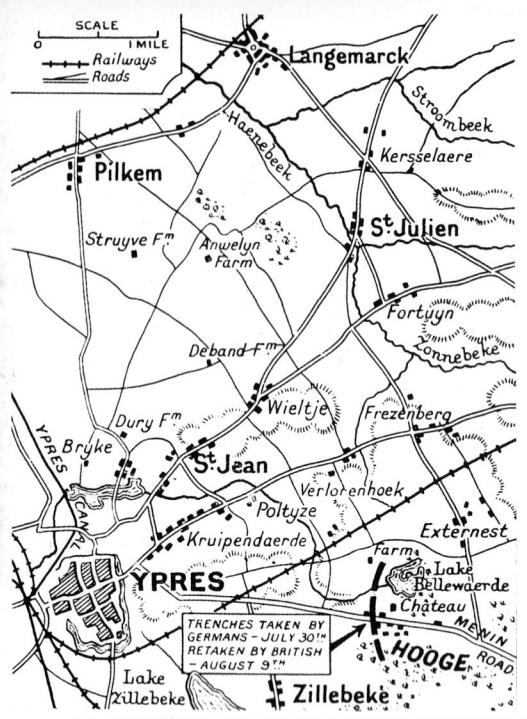

15GW652 The ground at Hooge torn by shell fire.

15GW655 Men of the Liverpool Scottish occupying the German trench at Bellewaarde Farm, Hooge, 16 June 1915.

15GW656 Crater left when a British mine was blown-up under the German positions at Hooge.

15GW654 The Liverpool Scottish attacking the German lines at Bellewaarde Farm. The banner signals the limit of the British advance.

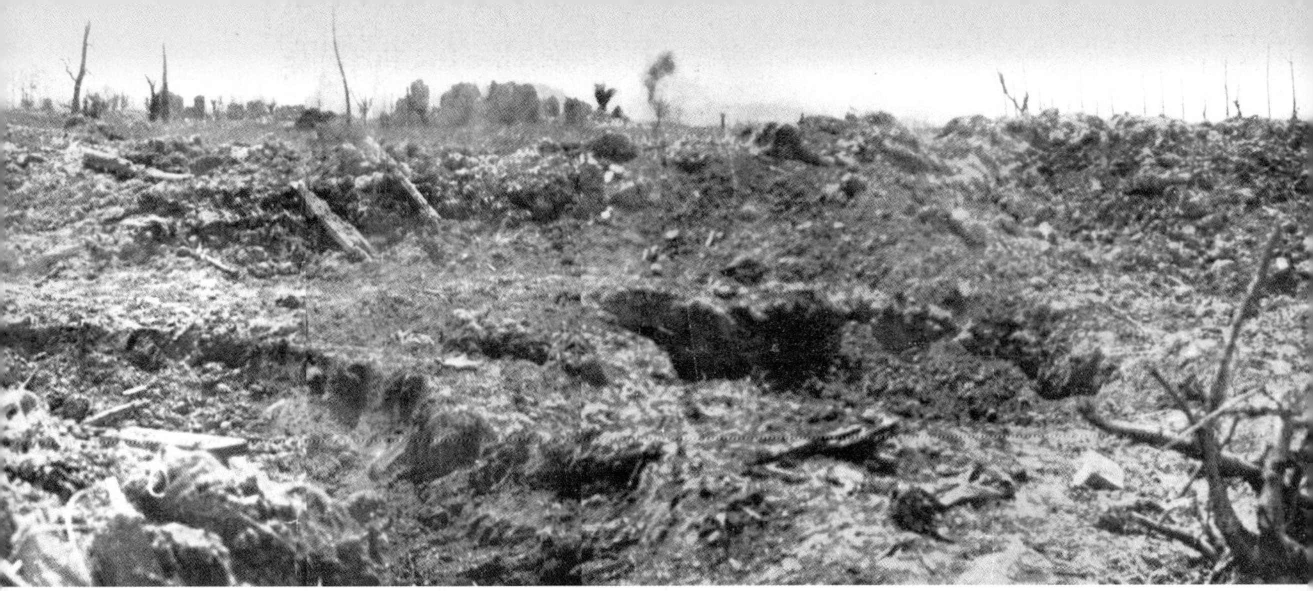

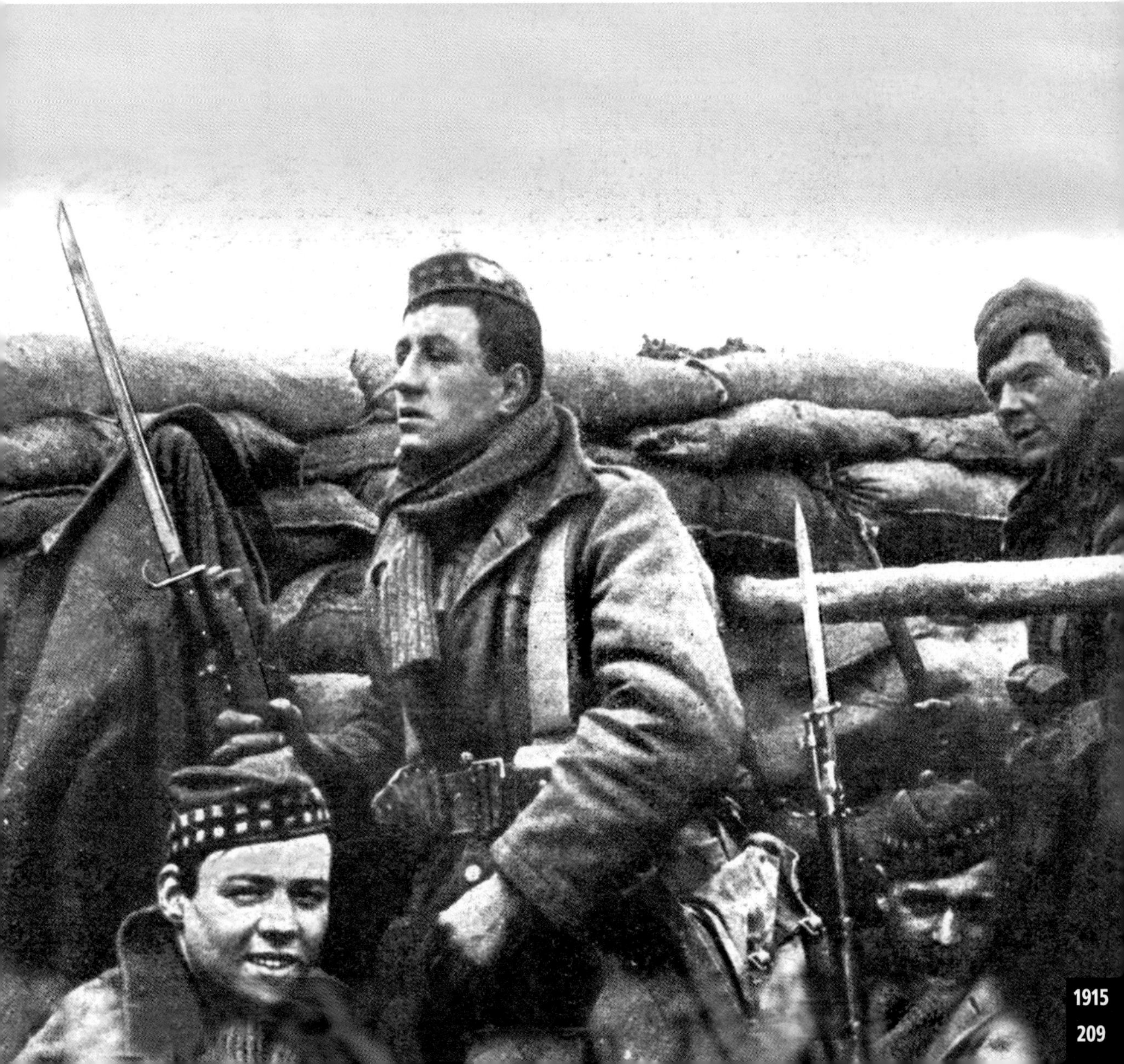

15GW668 British troops marching through wooded country to the trenches.

15GW659 British troops with a trench mortar

15GW660 A Vickers machine gun being operated in Sanctuary Wood.

15GW661 British troops with a trench oven.

15GW662 Painting trench sign posts.

15GW663 Dead Germans.

15GW658 The business end of a British trench.

15GW657 Germans cut down during a counter-attack.

15GW774 British officers in a dugout near Ypres with the walls decked with pictures taken from the *Sketch* magazine of the famous French actress and singer Gabrielle Deslys.

15GW776 15GW777 Officers and men of the 7th Battalion King's Own Scottish Borderers in Flanders.

15GW775 A German 'Jack Johnson' shell exploding amongst farm buildings in the British lines.

15GW778 Officers and men of the 1/5 Battalion York and Lancaster Regiment about to set off for the trenches near Fleurbaix. They are, left to right: Sergeant Major Lumb, C Company; Captain Mallinson; Captain Hugh Parry-Smith, C Company; Captain Johnson, B Company, and Captain Willis, A Company. Two unidentified officers' servants are standing behind in the doorway.

1915
213

15GW734 British officers of the 1/5 Battalion, York and Lancaster Regiment wearing early gas protection. This battalion had arrived in the Salient shortly before the first gas attack in April 1915. The tubes on the right are rockets to be fired in the event of an attack.

15GW736 A German work detail marching to the trenches near Ypres. Note the waders and bandoliers of extra ammunition.

15GW735 The beginning of the Ypres Salient in the north and the extreme point of the entire British Army in Flanders in 1915. The armies of three nations came together at this place: French soldiers occupied trenches on the left bank of the drained Yser Canal, starting near the large trees; opposite them were the Germans and the British. The 'X' marks where the German front line began and the dot the British. At this point the opposing British and German trenches were about ten to twelve yards apart in places. The 1/5th Battalion of the York and Lancaster Regiment manned this hot spot for a period in the summer of 1915, when the photographs were taken.

15GW740 Where the French and British lines met on the banks of the Yser.

15GW751 Rotherham men of A Company, 1/5 Battalion York and Lancaster Regiment. At this point in the line No Man's Land was only a few yards wide. Two of the men are armed with rifle grenades.

15GW739 The drained Yser Canal, with a flimsy bridge of planks for infantry to cross the mud.
15GW746 *Chevaux de frises* barbed wire obstacles guarding the British trenches. The German front line is on the horizon.

15GW743 Lieutenant Harry Colver, 1/5th Battalion, York and Lancaster Regiment, took a series of photographs of exceptional quality before he was killed in a phosgene gas attack on 19 December 1915. Above he is seen in International Trench (identified by Jon Cooksey), which had been captured recently from the Germans.

15GW741 1/5th Battalion, York and Lancaster Regiment's HQ with Colonel Fox (centre, with moustache) and some of his officers.

15GW738 North Zwaanhoff Farm on the east bank of the Yser Canal had been reduced to rubble by the German artillery (identified by Jon Cooksey). This position was close to where the Ypres Salient began in the north. At the time this photograph was taken by Lieutenant Harry Colver, the 1/5th Battalion, Yorks and Lancaster Regiment, was occupying this section of the line.

15GW742 Captain George Hewitt (left) at the entrance to his dugout in the Yser Canal sector. Lieutenant Colver on the right and Lieutenant Cattle in the middle.

15GW771 Captain Colver's men, A Company, relaxing in the fire trench at Fleurbaix.

15GW747 Dugouts at Fleurbaix. The man seated has taken the wire stiffener out of his hat and re modelled it to resemble a civilian flat cap of the day.

1915
219

15GW750 Men of the York and Lancs on the Yser Canal.

15GW744 Lieutenant Hess poses by a shell case which serves as an alarm in the event of a gas attack.

15GW721 View looking towards the German lines from the Second Line; the line of sandbags across the centre is a recently captured German trench which presently serves at the British Front Line; across No Man's Land is the German Front Line.

15GW745 View of the British rear area on the Yser Canal taken from a communication trench.

15GW749 Men of the York and Lancs on the Yser Canal.

15GW770 View looking towards the German positions from the parapet of International Trench. The ruined farm – Farm 14 – was immediately behind the German Front Line. A British attack on 6 July failed to capture this stronghold. There are some grave markers to the left, alongside what was the communication trench connecting International Trench with the German Second Line.

1915
223

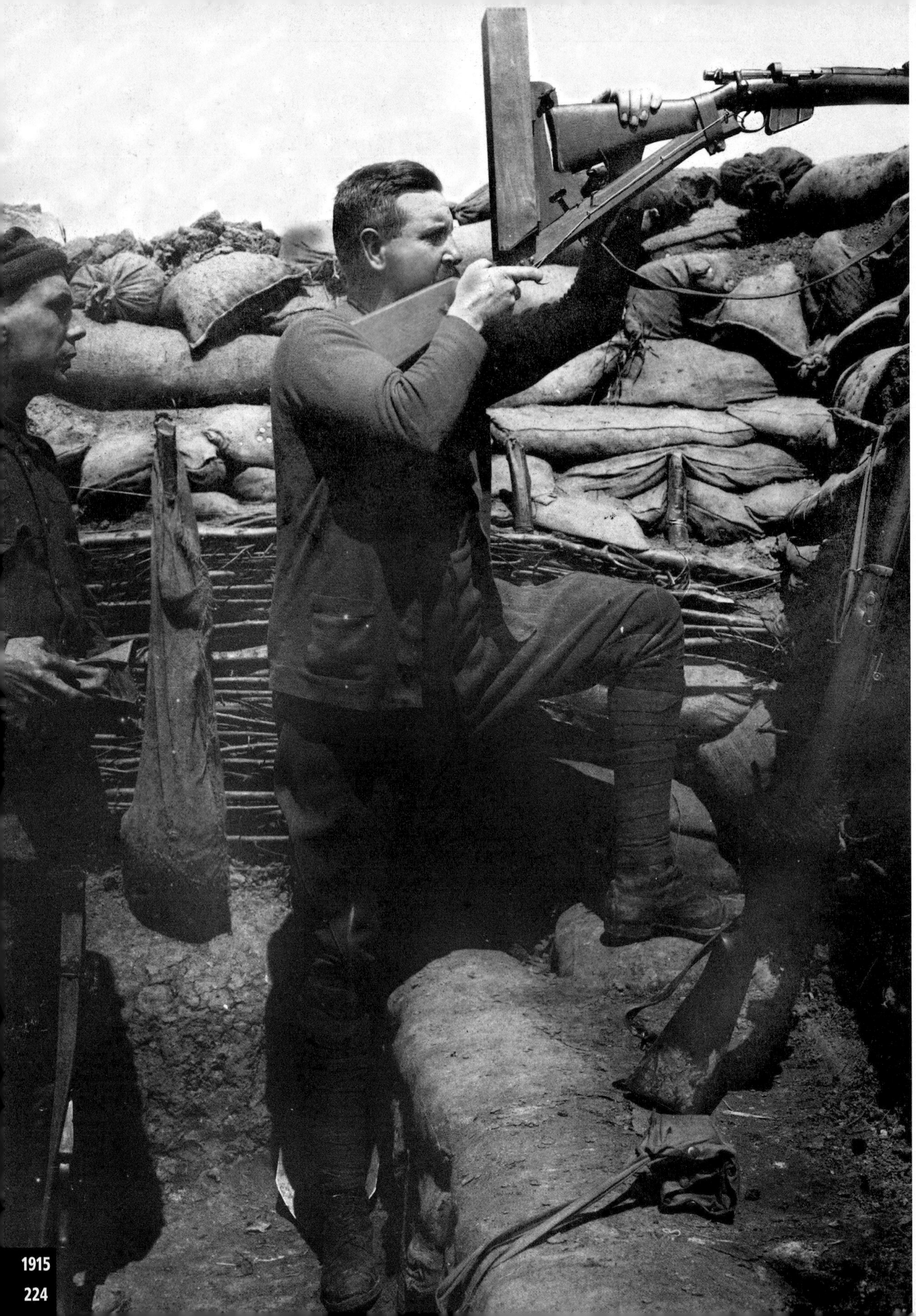

15GW772 Captain Hugh Parry-Smith, officer commanding C Company based at Birdwell Drill Hall, Barnsley, pre war, sighting up through a periscope with a rifle attached.

15GW748 View taken by Lieutenant Colver of Farm 14 through a periscope. The German Front Line can be seen as a line of sandbags to its front.

15GW769 German infantry preparing a farm building for defence.

15GW729 One of two German trench mortars captured by the British in an attack in September 1915. The two officers, Captain Rideal, Machine Gun Officer with the 1/5th Battalion, York and Lancaster Regiment and its Adjutant, Captain Parkinson, are in a destroyed part of International Trench. The weapon is a 91 mm Lanz *minenwerfer* and was first employed by the Germans at the beginning of the year. This particular one was shipped back to England by Lieutenant Harry Colver and was displayed at the Regimental HQ at Rotherham.

Information used in this chapter was based on the following titles in the **Battleground Europe** series of guide books: **Ypres – Sanctuary Wood and Hooge** and **Ypres – Hill 60** by Nigel Cave. See also **Flanders 1915** by Jon Cooksey in the **Images of War** series. These are available from Pen & Sword History Books Ltd.

Chapter Five: Zeppelin Attack – Incentives to Join The Colours

15GW794 *Deutsch Marineluftschiffabteilung* (German Naval Airship Division) on a raid, 1915.   **15GW784** A German artist's version of an attack on London.

15GW795 Ferdinand Adolf Heinrich August Graf von Zeppelin; born July 1838, died March 1917.

In days to come my airships are destined to erase the advantages or disadvantages of the geographical location of nations. For Germany, as the power most capable of supplying proficient crews, they will assure her world military domination, as indeed they will cause a complete revolution in commerce and transportation.'
      Graf von Zeppelin

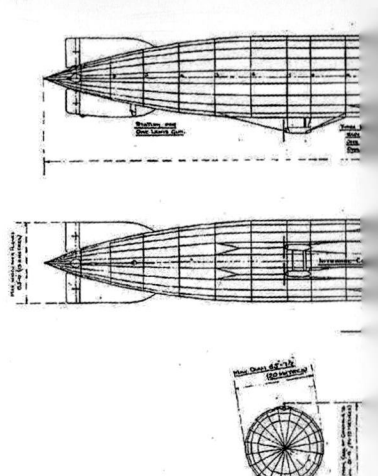

15GW781 Airship *LZ4* in her shed.

15GW783 *LZ1* coming in to land on Lake Constance.

15GW802 *LZ3* coming in to land and without disturbing the grazing sheep.

15GW800 *LZ2* at her mooring on Lake Constance.

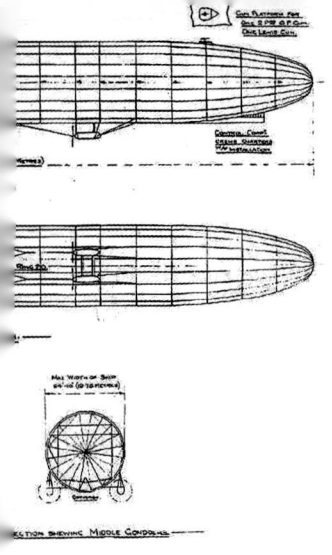

15GW780 The first flight of the *LZ1* in July 1900, taking off from Lake Constance. It remained airborne for twenty minutes and was considered a failure, but the design was improved upon.

15GW799 The *LZ3* lifting off stern first with crowds gathering to wave to its passengers.

15GW798 Count Zeppelin in the gondola of *LZ3*.

15GW779 Graf von Zeppelin.

15GW789 The Zeppelin *Victoria Luise* as a pre-war transporter of passengers.

15GW789 The *Sachsen* – Count Zeppelin played host on this occasion when the King of Saxony and his sons took a flight in this emerging form of transport.

15GW793 A close up of the stern of *LZ3* showing its control and stabalizing fittings – 1910.

15GW798 The rear gondola of *LZ3*.

15GW796 *LZ3* and her hanger on Lake Constance.

15GW801 Graf von Zeppelin takes his sister for a flight.

15GW788 A novelty in the skies above Germany in the years leading to war.

1915
231

15GW816 Count Zeppelin with the King of Saxony in the central gondola of an airship.

15GW814 The L 3 participated in the first raid on England on 19 January 1915. On 17 February 1915 L 3 was abandoned by its crew after a forced landing in Denmark. The wind blew the unmanned airship over the sea, where it was wrecked.

15GW815 A Zeppelin flying above the Belgian capital, Brussels, in 1915.

15GW807 The forward control gondola of a German naval airship, showing the electrical bomb release switches.

15GW802 A Zeppelin engine.

15GW787 The rear gondola, showing the engine controlling the rudder.

15GW817 A Zeppelin discharging water ballast from one of its gondolas.

15GW813 *Kapitänleutnant* Heinrich Mathy was known as the most daring and audacious of all the Zeppelin raiders.

1915

15GW808 The quick-firing French 75 mm field gun seen here mounted in the anti-aircraft role being examined by naval officers. This gun was in action against Zeppelin *LZ15* on the night of 13 October 1915.

15GW805 Ground crew run to take hold of the handling bars to assist landing this improved model airship in late 1915. It carried a crew of nineteen and could lift a load of 4,400 lbs of bombs. The front of the control car is to the left.

15GW806 The German battleship SMS *Markgraf* being overflown by Zeppelin *L54*.

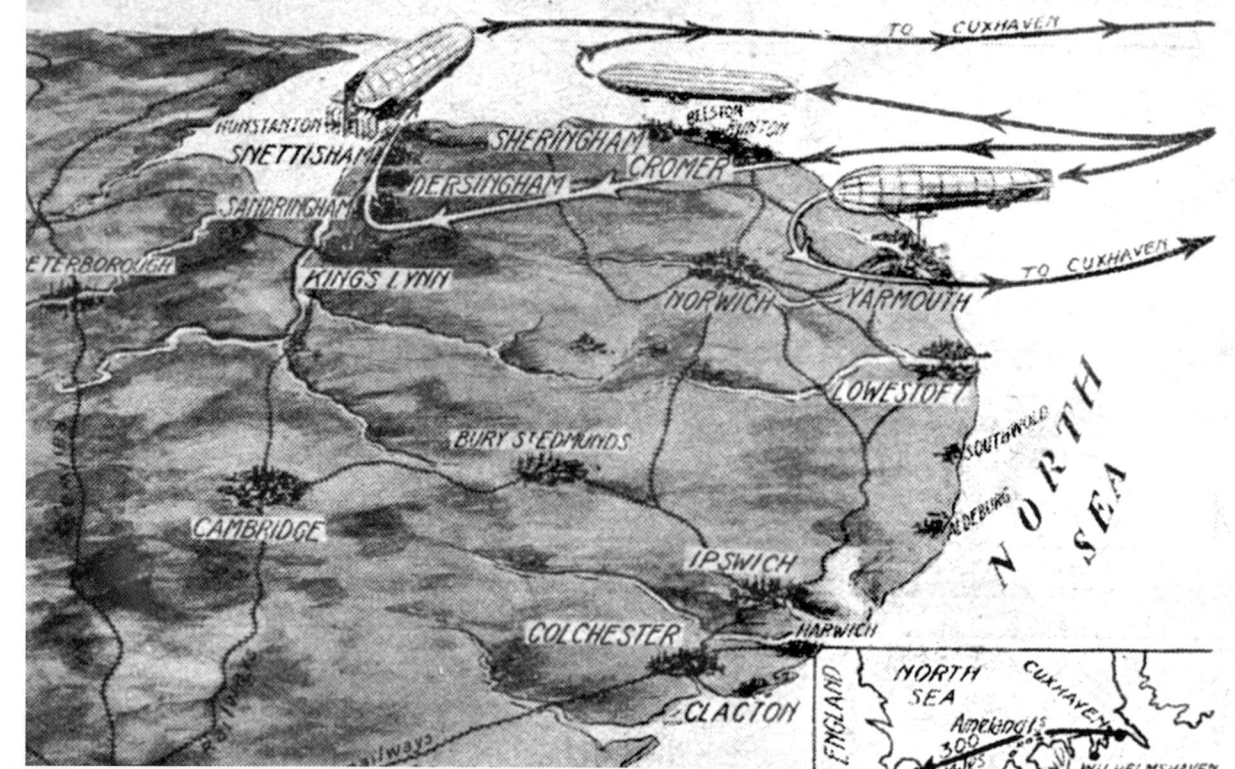

15GW822 Zeppelin bombs were dropped on Great Yarmouth on the first air raid made on Britain, 19 January 1915. The one on the left failed to explode.

15GW821 Mrs Gazeley, killed by a Zeppelin bomb in Yarmouth, 19 January 1915, photographed with her husband, who had been killed fighting in Flanders.

15GW841 Soldiers of the Norfolk Regiment among the ruins of a house destroyed at Great Yarmouth, 19 January 1915. The first air raid victims in Britain were killed in this raid. Martha Taylor and Samuel Smith were killed by a bomb which landed in the street.

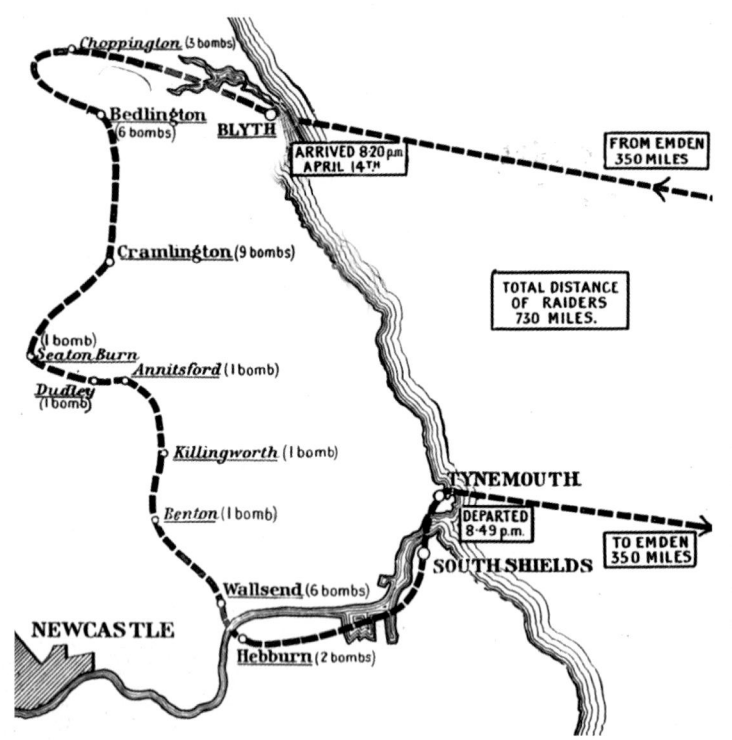

15GW819 & 15GW820 Zeppelin raider routes over north coast targets as presented to British magazine readers in 1915.

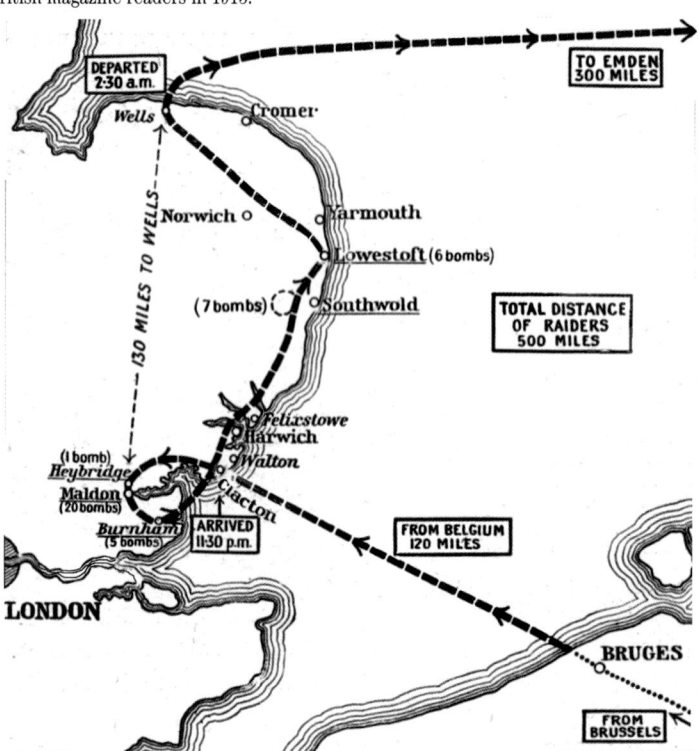

15GW828 15GW829 Zeppelin bombs dropped on Bury St Edmunds – a dud and a successful incendiary device.

15GW827 Officers and non commissioned officers of a Zeppelin after being awarded the Iron Cross for a raid over enemy territory (date and which territory not known).

15GW830 Varieties of ordnance dropped from Zeppelins on targets in England.

15GW832 Showing off the bombs.

15GW831 Bombs dropped during the raid on Bury St Edmunds in April 1915.

15GW836 Incendiary bomb dropped on Lowestoft.

15GW837 Incendiary bombs dropped over the Tyne.

15GW839 Loss of life at Yarmouth, St Peter's Plain, where Samuel Smith, shoemaker, was killed.

15GW838 Destruction at King's Lynn following the Zeppelin raid of the night of 19 January 1915.

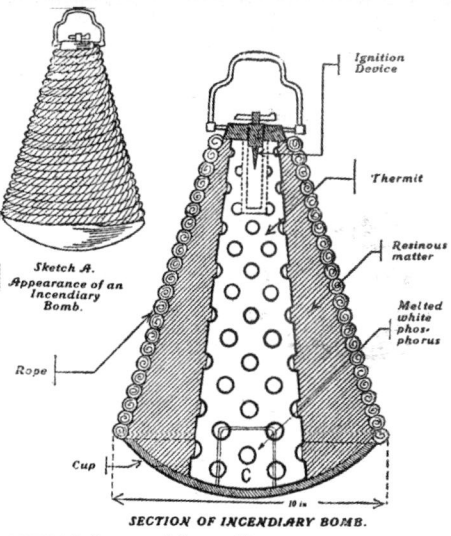

15GW834 A diagram of the workings.

15GW833 Showing off the bombs.

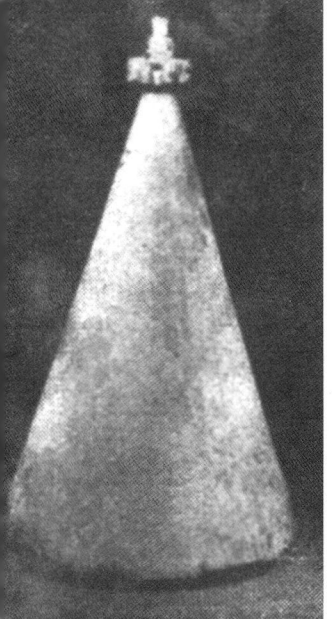

15GW840 High explosive bomb that failed to explode.

15GW835 One of the hated 'Baby Killers' that threatened life and limb of civilians, mainly along the north east coast of England and London.

1915
243

15GW826 Butter Market, Bury St Edmunds 30 April 1915.

15GW824 One of the bombs dropped on King's Lynn being examined by the Chief Constable, Charles Hunt.

15GW842 Soldiers helping with the salvaging of belongings in the bomb damaged house in King's Lynn.

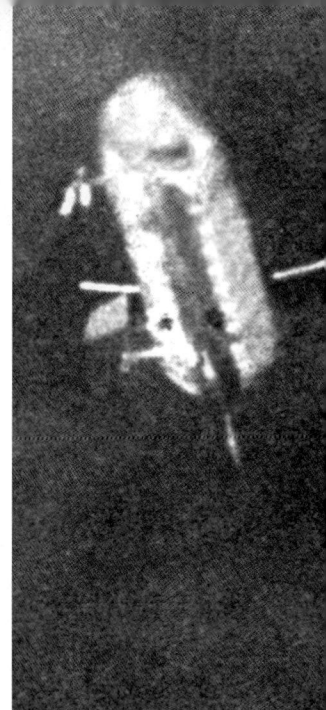

15GW786 Zeppelin *LZ15* commanded by *Kapitänleutnant* Breithaupt over London on the night of 13 October 1915. It was one of a number of airships raiding England that night. Casualties were 71 killed and 130 injured. An official statement the following day said: *The War Office announce that a fleet of hostile airships visited the Eastern Counties and a portion of the London area last night and dropped bombs. Anti-aircraft guns of the Royal Field Artillery, attached to the Central Force were in action. An airship was seen to heel over on its side and drop to a lower altitude. Five aeroplanes of the Royal Flying Corps went up.*

15GW843 Workers repairing damage to the road in Liverpool Street, London. Liverpool Railway Station had been the target on the night of 9 September 1915, when four bombs were dropped from Zeppelin *L13*: one landed on the station and three in the streets, killing fifteen people.

15GW844 Soldiers and civilians gathered around a burning gas main in Wellington Street, London. Zeppelin *LZ15,* commanded by *Kapitänleutnant* Breithaupt, dropped a bomb at this spot, killing seventeen people, 13 October 1915. The gas pipe under the street was fractured and caught fire.

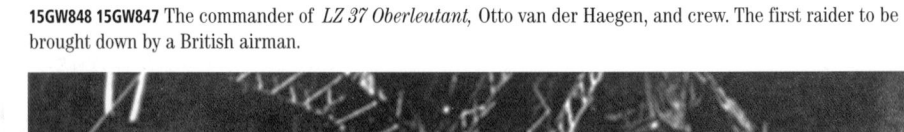

15GW848 15GW847 The commander of *LZ 37 Oberleutant,* Otto van der Haegen, and crew. The first raider to be brought down by a British airman.

15GW846 *LZ 37* over Zeppelin sheds.

15GW872 The French built Morane-Saulnier 'Parasol' scout with which Flight Sub-Lieutenant Warneford destroyed Zeppelin *LZ 37*.

15GW845 Flight Sub-Lieutenant Warneford RNAS destroyed Zeppelin *LZ 37* by getting above it and dropping six bombs, one of which brought the airship down in flames. He was awarded the Victoria Cross but was killed in an air accident two weeks later, on 17 June 1915.

15GW851 Edith Cavell in England, about years before the Great War.

Before the war, Nurse Edith Cavell was matron of a nursing school in Brussels. Prior to the outbreak of hostilities she was a training nurse for three hospitals in Belgium. She was arrested on 3 August 1915. At her court martial she was prosecuted for aiding British and French soldiers, in addition to young Belgian men, to cross the border and eventually enter Britain. She admitted her guilt in a statement prior to the trial. Her admission confirmed that Cavell had helped enemy soldiers to cross the Dutch frontier and clearly established that she helped them escape to a country at war with Germany. The penalty according to German military law was death.

15GW853 Edith Cavell in a garden in Brussels with her two dogs before the outbreak of the war.

15GW852 Belgian nursing school *École belge d'infirmières diplômées* – was founded in 1907. Direction of the School was entrusted to Nurse Edith Cavell.

15GW850 Cavell (seated centre) with a group of multinational student nurses whom she trained in Brussels.

The German government maintained that it had acted fairly towards Edith Cavell. In an official statement to the press, the German government stated that: *It was a pity that Miss Cavell had to be executed, but it was necessary. She was judged justly. It is undoubtedly a terrible thing that the woman has been executed; but consider what would happen to a State, particularly in war, if it left crimes aimed at the safety of its armies to go unpunished because they were acts committed by a woman.*

GW15855 German officials appointed by the German Government to administer affairs in occupied Belgium.

Front row sitting (left to right): Privy Councillor Major von Lumm; *Rittmeister* von der Lanken; Chief Administrator Dr von Sandt; Privy Councillor *Hauptmann* Mehlhorn; Privy Councillor Dr Bittmann.

Second row standing (left to right): Prince George von Sachsen-Meiningen; Councillor *Leutnant* Kempf; Dr Felix Somary; Privy Councillor *Leutnant* Bornhardt; *Rittmeister* Bücking; Bank Manager *Leutnant* Gutleben; *Rittmeister* Count Harrach; Acting Councillor von Radowitz; Administration Councillor Hauptmann von Wussow; Administrator and Surveyor of Buildings Degener; Bank Manager Dr Schacht; Councillor of Justice Schauer.

Third row (left to right): Privy Councillor *Hauptmann* Pochhammer; *Leutnant* Baron von Stein; Assistant Judge von Friedberg; Assistant Judge Schäffer; Herr Schotthöfer; Dr Ried; Leutnant Dr Hütten; Dr Böninger; *Leutnant* Honigmann; Councillor of Justice Trimborn; Herr Georg Behrens; Administration Councillor Löblich; Privy Councillor Brückner; Public Prosecutor *Leutnant* Bluhme; Rittmeister Prince zu Ratibor und Corvey; *Burgomeister Leutnant* von Loebell; Privy Councillor Rittmeister Kaufmann.

Fourth row (left to right): Herr Treutler; Dr Loymayer; Consul Dr Asmis; Assistant Judge Dr. Reuthner; Professor Rathgen.

15GW852 The Belgian nursing school *École belge d'infirmières diplômées* – was founded in 1907. Direction of the School was entrusted to Nurse Edith Cavell. It was here that Edith Cavell helped organize British, French and Belgian soldiers to escape into neutral Holland.

15GW860 Following the execution of Nurse Cavell on 12 October 1915, postcards and magazine articles flooded out in the countries ranged against Germany. This is a French depiction of her arrest and trial. She had been betrayed by Gaston Quien, who was later convicted by a French court as being a collaborator.

1915
251

15GW858 St Giles Prison, Brussels, where Cavell was held and executed.

15GW859 German soldiers quartered in the Cour d'Appel, The Palace of Justice, Brussels, at the beginning of the occupation of Belgium.

15GW858 The cell in St Giles Prison, Brussels, where Edith Cavell was held for ten weeks, the last two in solitary confinement.

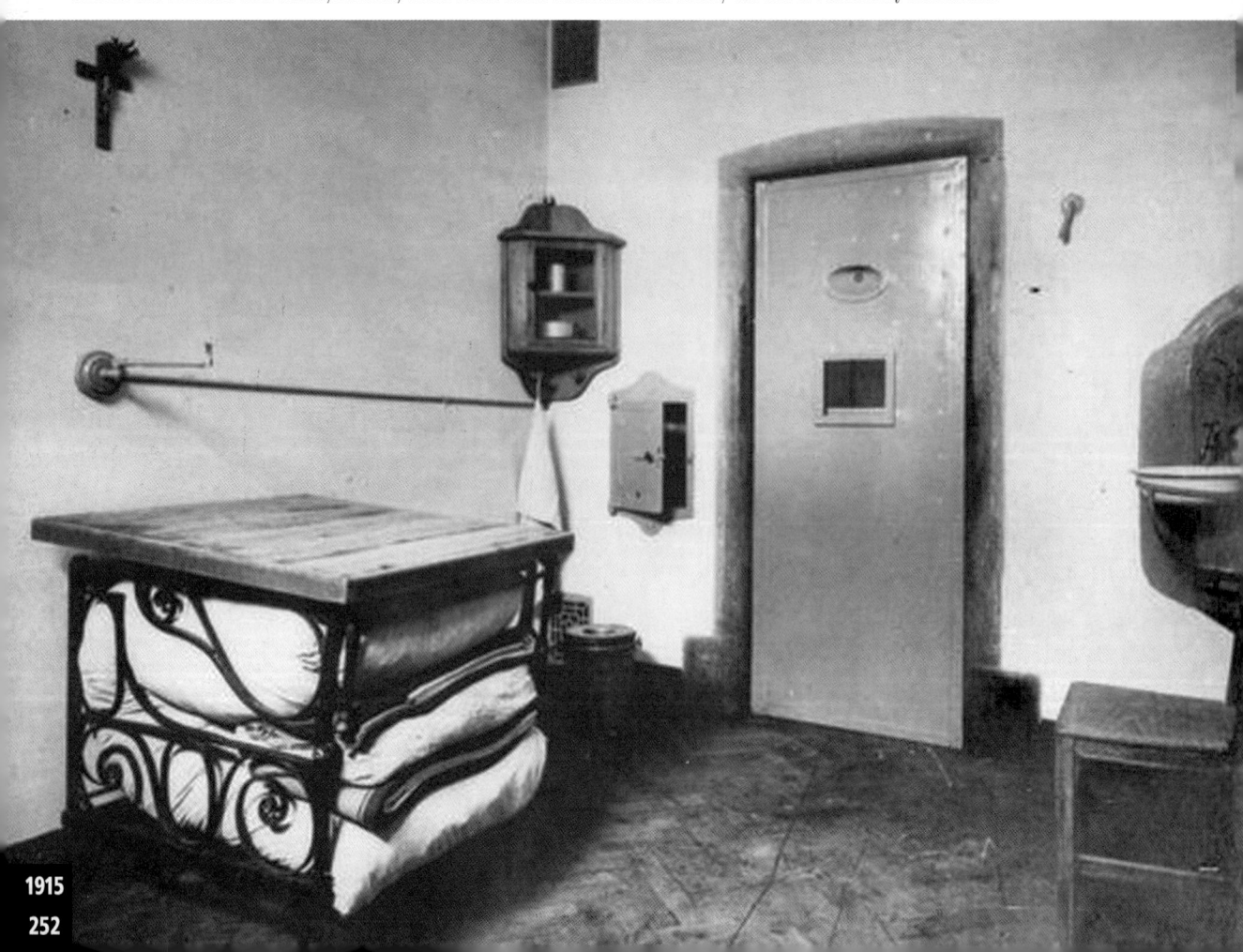

1915
253

15GW857 American diplomat, Hugh Simons Gibson, First Secretary of the United States Legation,
'*We reminded the German civil governor, Baron von der Lancken, of the burning of Louvain and the sinking of the Lusitania and told him that this murder would rank with those two affairs and would stir all civilised countries with horror and disgust.*'

15GW856 American Minister to Belgium, Brand Whitlock, wrote an appeal letter to the German Governor General of Belgium, Baron von Bissing:
'*She has spent her life alleviating the sufferings of others and at her school numerous nurses have been trained who, throughout the world, in Germany as in Belgium, have watched at the bedside of the sick. Miss Cavell gave her services as much to German soldiers as to others.*'
The Americans could intervene because in 1915 they were still neutral.

15GW864 Governor-General of occupied Belgium, *Generaloberst* Moritz von Bissing, as supreme authority, *Gerichtscherr*, ratified Nurse Edith Cavell's death warrant and refused to see a deputation from representatives of the American and Spanish governments.

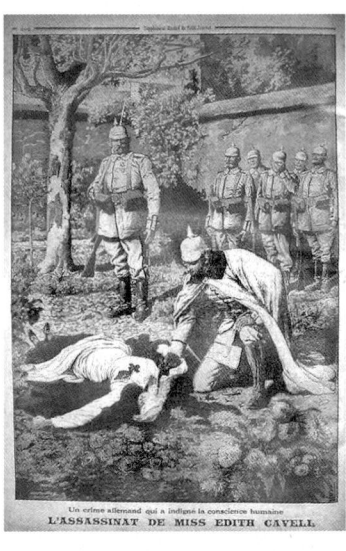

15GW862 Nurse Edith Cavell was born 4 December 1865 and was executed by firing squad for treasonous acts against the German occupying forces on 12 October 1915.

15GW863 The Head of the Political Department, Baron von der Lancken, received a delegation from the Hugh Simons Gibson, First Secretary of the United States Legation, who was accompanied by the Spanish Minister, Marquis de Villobar. Baron von der Lancken telephoned the Military Governor, Moritz von Bissing. Lancken conveyed the final decision to the American and Spanish diplomats:
'I have acted in the case of Miss Cavell only after mature deliberation; that the circumstances in her case were of such a character that I considered the infliction of the death penalty imperative; and that in view of the circumstances of this case I must decline to accept your plea for clemency, or any representation in regard to the matter.'
The execution was carried out the next morning, 12 October 1915.

15GW867 A British propaganda stamp issued shortly after Cavell's death.

15GW866 One of the many artists' impressions of the execution. The ... nt was a gift to those involved in waging the propaganda war ... inst the Germans.

15GW865 The Governor General of Belgium, Baron Moritz Bissing, on the steps of the Cathedral in Brussels. With him is the Archbishop of Munich, Cardinal Bettinger, who has just conducted the service. This was a few weeks after the execution.

15GW870 Londoners gathered in their thousands at a service in St Paul's Cathedral, London, to pay a last tribute of reverence to the memory of Miss Edith Cavell. An eye witness described the scene in the original caption:

'What a sight it was, statesmen, scholars, scientists, a great company of nurses in their various uniforms, pathetic groups here and there of wounded soldiers home from the battlefields and then an immense concourse of the general public, chiefly women. What had brought the multitude together?... the memory of a poor woman, a hospital nurse, who has been foully done to death by a barbarous enemy.'

15GW868 The German action was justified according to the rules of war; however, by not showing clemency and shooting Edith Cavell they committed a serious propaganda blunder. Within days the nurse became a martyr and, worldwide, the Germans were being described as 'monsters'. After her death was announced Allied determination was strengthened, and recruitment doubled during the next eight weeks.

15GW869 An artist's impression of the memorial service held in St Paul's Cathedral – note the central praying figure is that of a young attractive nurse looking heavenwards – she appears to be loosely based on the the figure in the photograph above. The entire execution incident was a gift to those wishing to stir up sympathy and patriotism. The prayer concocted for the occasion reflected the mood and involved the Almighty (who now, more than ever, could be viewed as favouring the Allies). In part it read: *'We give hearty thanks, for it hath pleased Thee to deliver Thy servant, Edith, out of the miseries of this sinful world.'* Incredibly, church attenders were encouraged to view her execution as some sort of a divinely ordained deliverance.

15GW871 In sharp contrast with the patriotism inflamed by the execution of Edith Cavell was this meeting six months earlier of the Women's Peace Congress held at the Hague. More than 1,200 delegates from twelve countries discussed proposals to end the Great War through negotiation. British organizers had planned an attendance by 180 women delegates but this was reduced to three by a refusal to issue travel documents and the British Government's suspension of ferry services between England and Holland at that time. Also the French government would not permit any of its nationals to attend. The original caption for this picture, which appeared in *The Illustrated War News*, 5 May 1915, read in part:

'The futile and foolish International Women's Congress at the Hague: a meeting which ended in "war". One episode, illustrated above, was a "pause in silent reverence for the dead," during which, we are told, "women wept, and the meeting was suspended until they could regain their composure".

Such caption writing conveys the utter contempt held for those who failed to go along with the patriotic spirit of the time. The incident of the would-be British delegates, being thwarted in their attempts to attended the Peace conference was referred to as *'almost amusing – it hardly created comic relief amid the world tragedy'*.

1915

15GW785 One immediate effect of the Zeppelin raids on London – the boost to recruiting was notable.

15GW810 Execution of British nurse Edith Cavell on 12th October 1915 was a gift to the recruiting drive.

15GW811 The Church of England added its voice for revenge against Germany. On Sunday 25 July 1915 the Bishop of London led a patriotic parade to St Paul's Cathedral, where he delivered a stirring sermon of hate to the London Territorials: *It is the soul of England which is once more to free the world,* he cried with fervour, from behind an altar made up of military drums.

1915
259

OUR FRIEND THE ENEMY.

JOHN BULL (*very calmly*). "AH, HERE HE COMES AGAIN—MY BEST RECRUITER."

Chapter Six: The New Army – The Armaments

15GW916 Practising shooting at the miniature range at the School of Musketry.

15GW917 The new type of warfare demanded guns and lots of shells. The British offensives of 1915 lacked both, especially shells.

UNDER LORD DERBY'S SCHEME A MERE PROMISE TO ENLIST IS OF NO VALUE.

If a man wishes to be placed in a Group he MUST BE ATTESTED BY DECEMBER 11th

In the autumn of 1915 the Director General of Recruiting, Edward Stanley, 17th Earl of Derby, introduced a scheme to establish whether British manpower goals could be met by volunteers or if conscription was necessary. Each man aged 18 to 41 was to make a declaration of availability. However, when the scheme was announced men went to the recruiting office without waiting to be called.

15GW925 Lord Derby's appeal for more men was met with enthusiasm, as seen here at this London recruiting office.

15GW926 A crowd of 1,500 men at in London at the Brixton Recruiting Office queue to be attested.

15GW927 Some of the large crowd who rushed to enlist during the final days of the Derby Scheme being sworn in. The oath taken was as follows:
I, ... NAME... swear by Almighty God, that I will be faithful and bear true Allegiance to His Majesty King George V, his Heirs and Successors, and that I will, as in duty bound, honestly and faithfully defend His Majesty, his Heirs and Successors, in Person, Crown, and Dignity, against all enemies, and will observe and obey all orders of His Majesty, His Heirs, and Successors, and of the Generals and Officers set over me. So help me God.

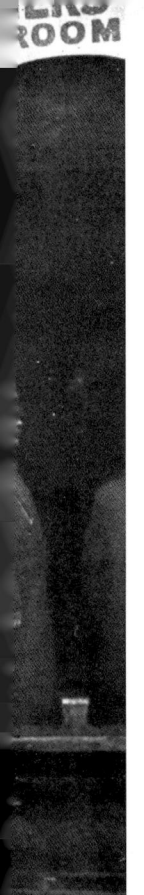

1915

15GW929 As the test period of Lord Derby's scheme drew near its end, volunteers besieged the recruiting offices. **15GW928** Southwark Town Hall.
15GW930 Midnight at a South London recruiting depot, where staff were kept busy into the night.

15GW931 Hammersmith Town Hall, where armbands are being distributed as confirmation of enlistment.

15GW932 When Derby Groups were called up they were generally allowed to chose the regiment in which they wished to serve. Sergeants from various regiments attended eager to secure the finest men for their own battalions.

15GW934 Men of the Royal Naval Division led by Commander the Hon. Rupert Guinness, marching through London to be reviewed by the Lord Mayor, who by virtue of his office was the Admiral of the Port of London.

15GW933 A recruiting gimmick outside the Royal Naval Division's office in the Strand, London. The idea was that a curious person would step up to view the 'Photograph of the man we want' only to discover that he is looking into a mirror. On hand were recruiters to help him make up his mind and sign him up for the Royal Naval Division.

15GW936 Recruiting underway in Trafalgar Square and the camera captures the moment when a candidate for the army, persauded by the retoric, is helped up on to the platform to sign up.

15GW935 Outside the Mansion House, London, 'Armleteers' studying the first proclamation listing the four Derby Groups who have been called to the Colours.

1915
267

BRACES

RIFLE

RIGHT AMMUNITION-POUCHES

LEFT AMMUNITION-POUCHES

BELT

ENTRENCHING TOOLS

WATER-BOTTLE

BAYONET

HAVERSACK

ENTRENCHING TOOL HANDLE

BALACLAVA HELMET

HOUSEWIFE

HOLDALL

1915
268

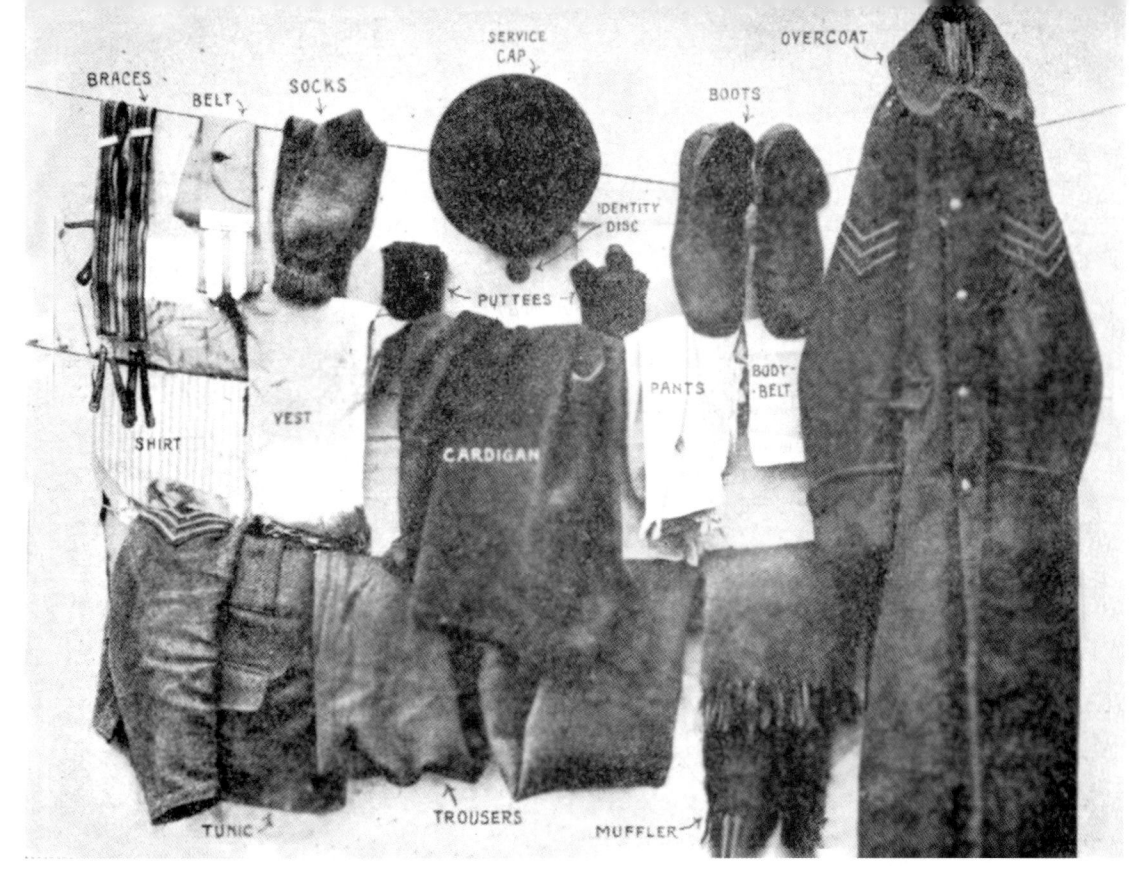

15GW932/15GW933/15GW931 A British soldier's equipment as issued to every infantry soldier. These illustrations appeared in the Illustrated War News in 1915. The oddly named 'housewife' is a buttons, needle and thread repair kit for darning socks and sewing on shirt buttons.

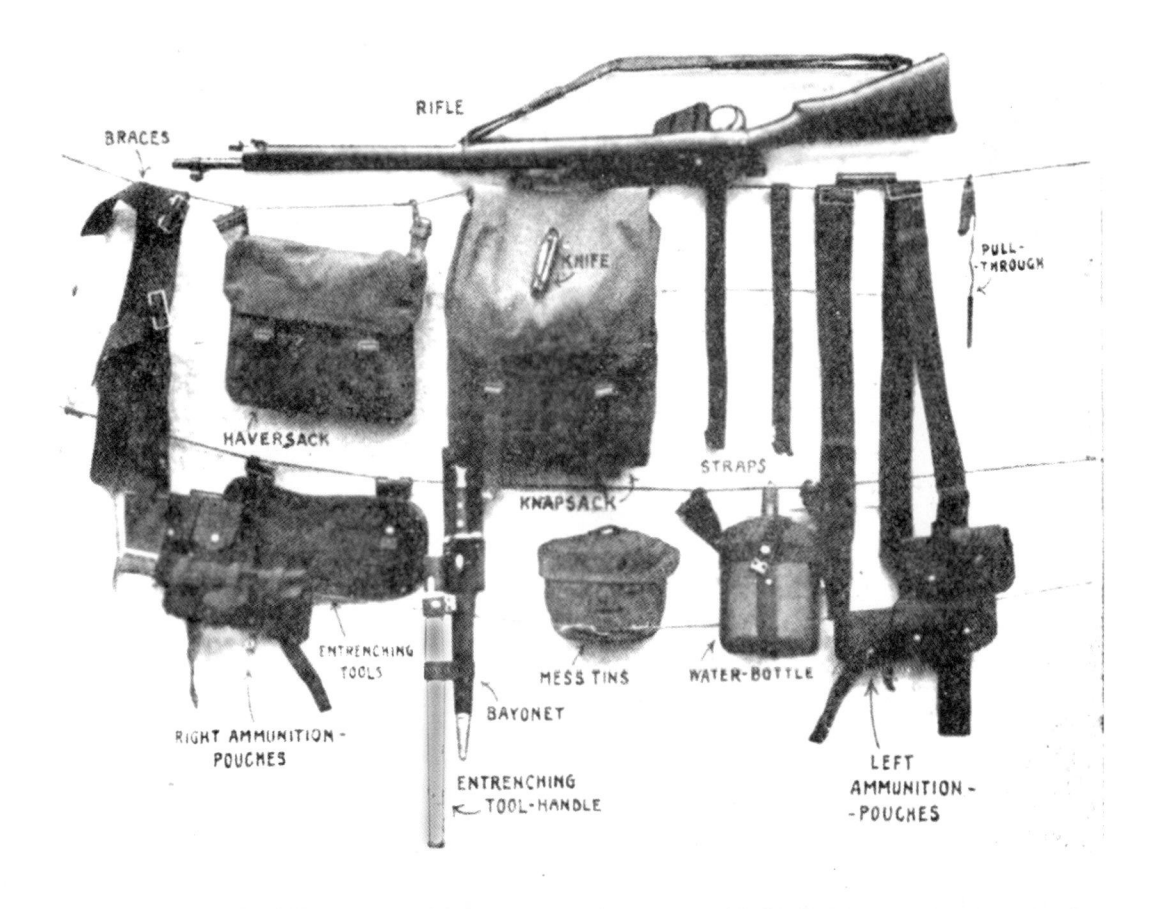

15GW1038/15GW1036/15GW1039/15GW1037 A new waterproof cape was designed to double as a rain protector and a groundsheet. It was made of a rubberized substance and when issued to British soldiers it became known as the 'gas cape'; it did provide some protection from German mustard gas. It was introduced in April 1915 and is modelled here by a corporal in the Honourable Artillery Company. The Germans became aware of its impending use by the British Army and issued the following order in October 1915 to its troops fighting on the Somme front:

The British War Office has approved the issue of a new type of overcoat for British troops. This garment can be used as a water-proof coat, sleeping bag, ground sheet, apron and valise cover. In case such a garment is found it is to be handed to Divisional Headquarters.

The Germans saw the need to evaluate the new piece of equipment. It went on to equip British soldiers throughout the Second Worlds War and after.

1915
271

15GW918 Men of the Royal Gloucestershire Regiment resting during a route march.

15GW919 Kit inspection of a Kitchener battalion at Cambridge.

15GW921 Recruits at physical drill, which will bring them to fighting fitness.

15GW922 Men of the New Army toning up their stomach muscles on the wall bars.

15GW924 Mock execution at a camp at St Albans.

15GW920 Kitchener soldiers stationed at Trinity College, Cambridge.
15GW923 Camp butchers with The Sportsman's Battalion (Royal Fusiliers) cutting up meat for dinner.

15GW1040/15GW1042/15GW1043/15GW1044/15GW1041 Boys from Eton College, near Windsor, helping the war effort by unloading a consignment of field guns. It was from among the ranks of such young men from public schools that many officers would be drawn in the next three years. By 1918 40% would be commissioned from the ranks.

1915

1915

15GW1045 Review of the Nationalist Volunteers in Phoenix Park, Dublin, Easter Sunday 1915. It was the first time that Ireland had collected armed forces under the control of its nationalist leaders with the blessing of the British Government.

15GW1046 The City of London Volunteer Corps (National Guard) at training during Easter holidays, April 1915, at Brighton. This is the morning nine o'clock parade.

15GW1048 The National Guard at musketry training, Brighton, May 1915. These middle-aged men appear to be holding their rifles at the slope in an unorthodox manner, apart from the man in the front rank, third from right who is holding his rifle in the drill book regulation manner, with the bolt uppermost.

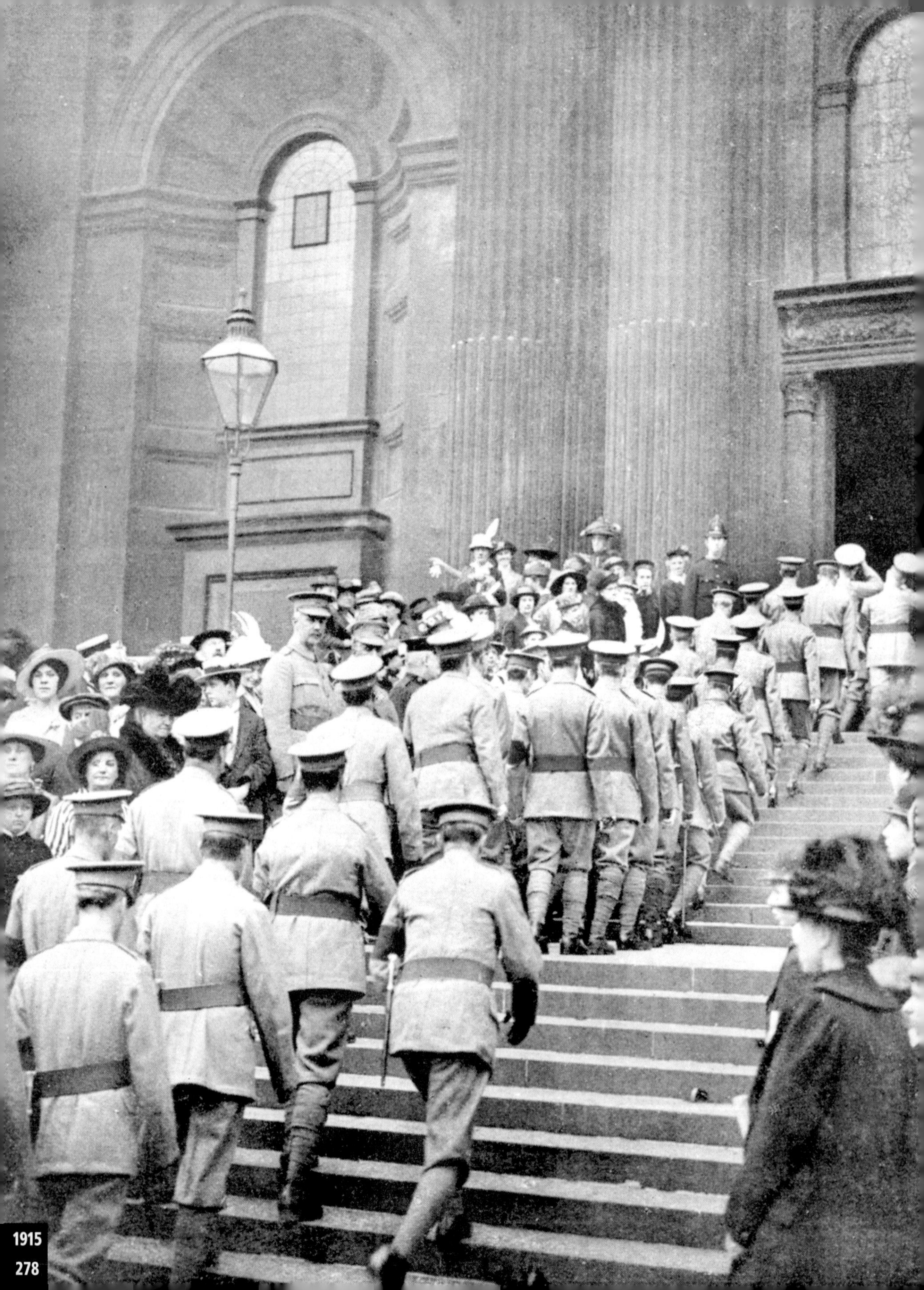

1915
278

15GW1047 St Paul's Cathedral, 9 June, 1915, men of the National Guard enter for a church service conducted by the Bishop of London, who told them:
'The National Guard is making boys of you all again and it is a step in the direction of the necessary organisation of national service.'

15GW1051 Elderly gentlemen of the National Guard engaged in digging trenches for the defence of London.

15GW1049 Quartmaster's staff at the National guard camp: R.Q.M.S Bartlett, Q.M.S. Uniacke, Co.Q.M.S. Courtney and Sergeant Newman.

15GW1050 Colonel Richard Kirby Ridgeway VC former officer in the Indian Army, was engaged as an advisor to the National Guard. He won his Victoria Cross during fighting on the North Eastern Frontier of India in 1879.

15GW1053 A firing range was set up at Portnall Park and was inaugurated at a luncheon given on 25 September 1915. Here some senior members of the Guard engage in shooting.

1915
279

15GW1056 The National Guard stand at a Summer Fair held 6-7 June 1915.

15GW1057 Alderman Sir Charles Johnson, Baronet, Lord Mayor of London 1915.

15GW1055 One of the duties carried out by men of the National Guard was the securing of London railway stations. The Station Company for King's Cross and St Pancras are seen here.

15GW1052 Men of the National Guard engaged in digging trenches for the defence of London.

15GW1059 The work of the Ambulance Section at Brighton.

15GW1058 The National Guard practice throwing hand grenades.

15GW1054 Soldiers back home on leave from the fighting and still caked in the filth of the trenches – no doubt infested with lice.

1915
281

15GW937 A photographer has come too close to British troops at their training and a sentry has called out the guard. A sergeant examines his papers.
15GW938 A camp kitchen at Aldershot.

15GW939 A cookhouse kitchen with cooks preparing a meal for hundreds of men.
15GW943 The finer points of digging a trench are being pointed out.

15GW944 A corporal in the Rifle Brigade demonstrates the correct way to load a charger clip (each holding five rounds) into the magazine of a Short Lee Enfield.

15GW940 Recruits at their early morning toilet.

15GW1060 London Territorials training for trench warfare across the Channel by learning how to launch bombs by means of a catapult.

15GW941 A Kitchener battalion gets used to digging trenches, under the gaze of civilian onlookers.

15GW948 NCOs familarising themselves with the newly issued Short Lee Enfield rifle.

15GW942 Diggers pause for, and pose for, the camera. Civilian dress is still in evidence among these recruits.

15GW1061 Prototype helmet made of manganese steel produced by Hadfield of Sheffield. It was not adopted by the British Army and the 'Brodie' type helmet was used instead. When Germany declared war on Portugal in March 1916 the 'jelly-mould' helmet was supplied to the Portuguese Army by the British.

15GW945 A corporal demonstrates how to hold and take aim with the rifle.

15GW1029 A plan of a trench system, illustrating the methods being employed in Flanders.

15GW949 On the range with the new rifle.

15GW947 How to use the sights on the Short Lee Enfield.

15GW1025 Demonstrating the use of the 'ultimate weapon' – the bayonet.

15GW950 Soldiers cleaning their rifles by pouring boiling water down the barrels prior to oiling them.

15GW1023 A patrol of Cylist scouts lying in ambush.

15GW1062 Creeping up on an 'enemy' position.

15GW1026 A Maxim machine gun section

1915
287

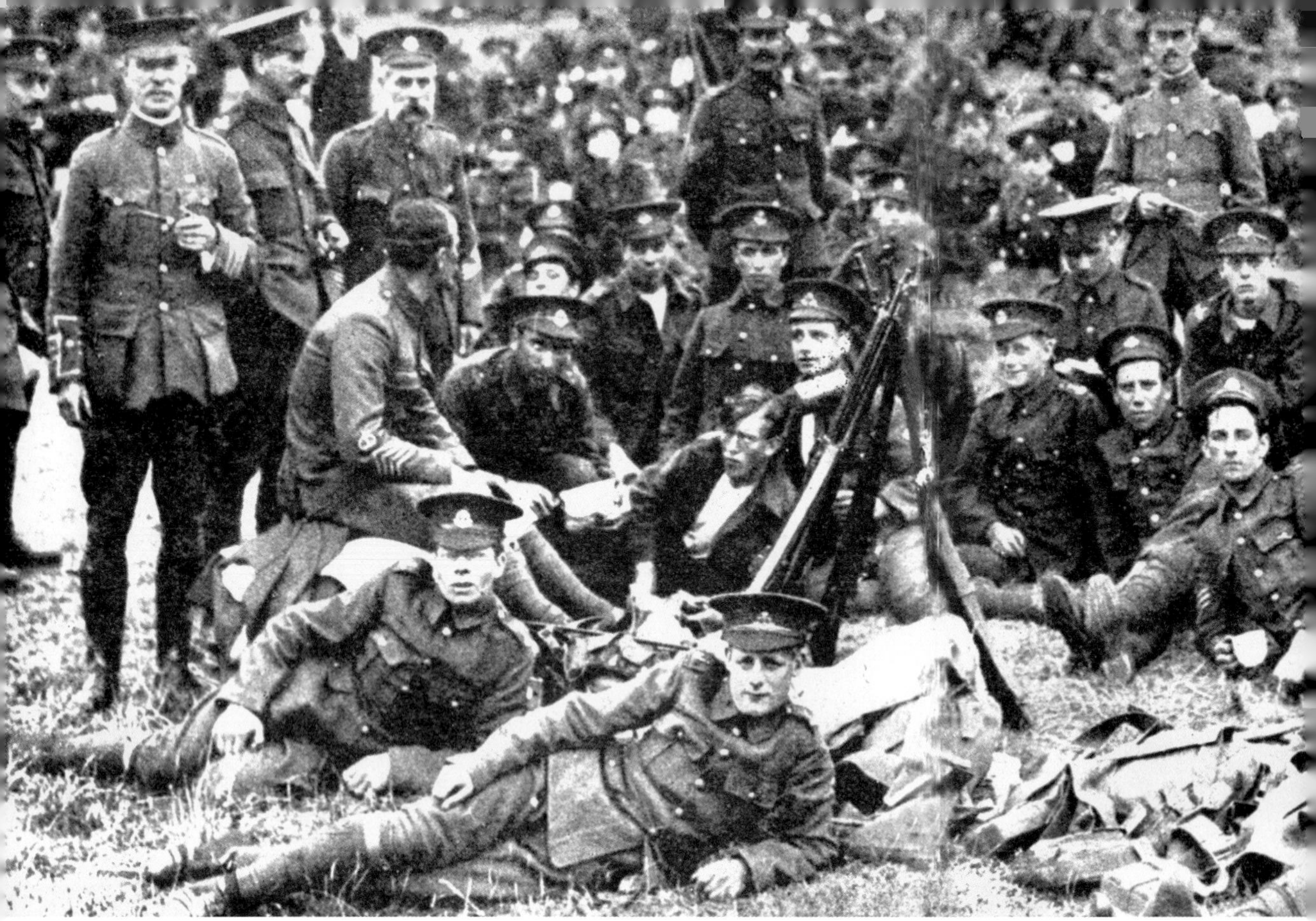

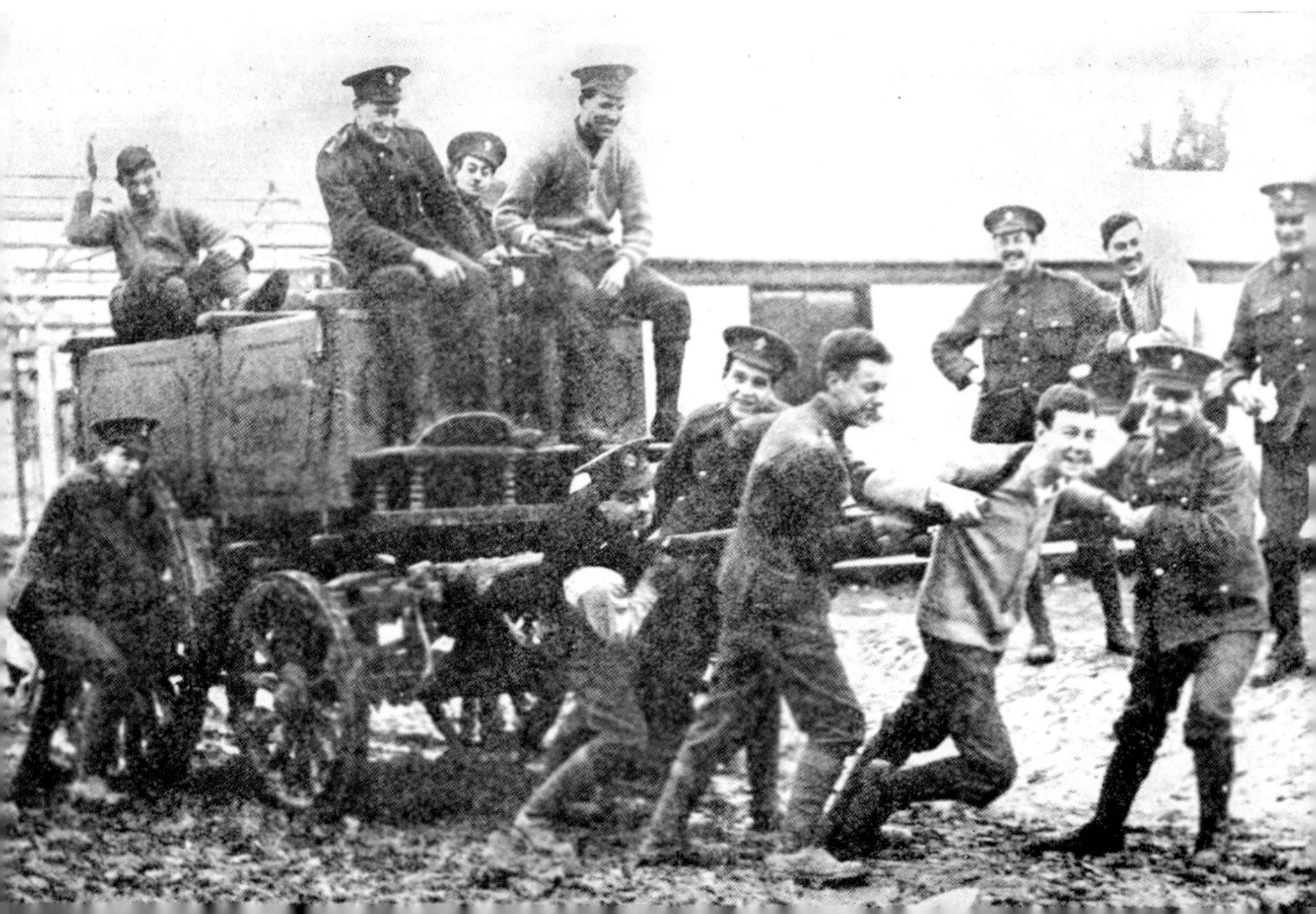

15GW1066 Recruits have their feet inspected after a route march.

15GW1065 A Kitchener battalion of the Middlesex Regiment waiting for the order to fall in for a route march.

15GW1064 Having fun bringing in the water wagon.

15GW1067 Men of 70 Infantry Brigade having dinner in a large marquee at Frensham Park, Surrey.

15GW1069/15GW1070/15GW1071 The 9th Battalion, North Staffordshire Regiment, practising building rafts and bridges.

15GW1063 A Company of a battalion of the Loyal North Lancashire Regiment, fully trained and ready for the fighting in France.

15GW1068 A despatch rider at signalling practice.

15GW1072 University and Public Schools Ambulance Corps on a field day at Epsom.

15GW1074 One method of removing a wounded man from the battlefield. His wounds are bandaged and then he is secured to the back of a mule.

15GW1073 A wounded man being brought in, supported on two rifles placed between two bicycles. One has to doubt the practicality of the arrangement.

15GW1075 Army transport driving at high speed through a ford.

15GW1079 How to load a wounded man onto a horse drawn ambulance wagon.

15GW1081 A Royal Army Medical Corps Field Hospital in the field, showing the kitchen and cooking facilities.

15GW1080 First Aid for the wounded – training for the fighting in France and Belgium, men of the Universities and Public Schools Brigade.

15GW1077 A British 18-pounder field gun, with a range of 7,000 yards, here being used in a training exercise.

15GW1076 Batteries of British 18-pounder field guns forming up to come into action.

15GW1078 A British 60-pounder field gun, with a range of 10,300 yards, being hauled into position.

Field Marshal Sir John French

Lieutenant Colonel Charles à Court Repington

'The reason why the British attack failed at Neuve Chapelle was a shortage of shells.' This comment by Field Marshal Sir John French to a close friend and war correspondant, Charles Repington, began a series of events that culminated in the removal of the Field Marshal and his replacement by Sir Douglas Haig several months later. On 14 May that conversation was reported in *The Times* in an article that quoted French as saying: 'We had not sufficient enough high explosives to lower the enemy's parapets to the ground. The want of an unlimited supply of high explosives was a fatal bar to our success.'

Casting about for those responsible caused opinion to finger the War Office and Lord Kitchener in particular, who, apparently, had failed to supply the ammunition required. David Lloyd George, then the Liberal Chancellor, was convinced that Kitchener was incapable of preparing the country's munitions factories for all-out war.

On 25 May the pressure brought about by the 'Shell Scandal' began to take effect. Herbert Asquith's Liberal government collapsed and a Ministry of Munitions was created under Lloyd George, who marginalised Kitchener. Lord Kitchener remained in office as Secretary of State for War, responsible for training and equipping the volunteer New Armies; he had however, now lost control over munitions production. Sir John French was also affected by his meddling in politics, a factor which contributed to his removal in December 1915. More factories began to be built across the country for the mass production of munitions. It was realized that if Britain and her allies were going to prevail against a determined enemy then an entire change in approach to the war would have to be adopted. Railway companies were engaged to produce guns and munitions in their engineering workshops.

Field Marshal Horatio Herbert Kitchener.

Chancellor of the Exchequer David Lloyd George

1915

15GW1089/1087 Women engaged in munition production: a social revolution had been forced on the western world by the scale of hostilities, as battles devoured men in alarming numbers and women were recruited to work in factories as well as all manner of jobs formerly held by the menfolk.

15GW1094 A young women operating a power lathe, turning crank shafts for lorry engines.

15GW1086 Testing shell cases for flaws in the casting by tapping with a hammer and noting the sound.

1915
301

1915

15GW1096/1093/1092/1090 Stages in the production of mortar bombs for firing from the British 2-inch trench mortar. The round bomb at the top of the shaft measured 9-inches in diameter and remained above the weapon before firing. Designs for both mortar and ammunition meant that they could be manufactured by small, unsophisticated workshops, unsuited to the production of larger weapons. Their introduction into the armoury of the British Army occurred in 1915 and would be used as a trench bombardment weapon for the next three years. In this series of photographs apprentices are being instructed in the manufacture of the projectiles, which were popularly referred to by the troops as 'toffee apples' or 'plum puddings'.

15GW1088/1083/1082/1085/1084 French shell producing factories increased production throughout 1915.

1915
305

15GW1097/1098/1099/1085/110
A nineteenth century invention to curb the movement of cattle in America, its usefulness in war was soon appreciated and was used in a belt of entanglements from the English Channel to the Swiss border. Here we see barbed wire being manufactured in France.

1915

15GW1101 Messrs. Vickers, Sons, and Maxim had promised to turn a number of ladies into proficient makers of shells and these volunteers, which included several titled women, are seen here at the Vickers works. They include: Lady Gertrude Crawford, Lady Gatacre and Lady Colebrook. The original caption noted: 'The work, curious as it may at first seem for women, is not unsuitable for them, as the work calls for that delicacy of manipulation which is a feminine instinct.'

1915
309

15GW737 As 1915 came to a close the British steel helmet began to appear and the design would remain largely unchanged for two world wars and beyond.

Chapter Seven: The Battle of Loos

15GW913 After reviling the Germans for using poison gas at Ypres, the British used gas for the first time at the Battle of Loos. An artist's impression of the charge.

15GW914 A street in Loos after the town's capture. The distinctive pithead gear, known as Tower Bridge, remained largely intact for a short while.

15GW906 Lord Kitchener and Mr Asquith entering a car en route for the conference between ministers of Britain and France and the two commanders-in-chief at Calais. The subject for discussion was: how best to drive the Germans out of French and Belgian territory before the end of 1915.

15GW907 French and British Naval Ministers; M. Augagneur, walking with Mr Balfour, First Lord of the Admiralty, Tuesday 6 July 1915, at the Calais conference.

15GW908 Calais Railway Hotel, 6 July 1915: the British Commander-in-Chief, Sir John French, in conversation with French General Huguet, Chief of the French Mission to the British Expeditionary Force.

15GW910 Colonel Fitzgerald and Field Marshal French seen leaving the hotel after the conference.

15GW909 General Joffre and Lord Kitchener go in to the conference together. The French Minister of Munitions, M. Albert Thomas, is on the left.

15GW911 Leaving the Hotel after the conference: M. Delcassé; M. Viviani, President of the Council; Lord Crewe and Lord Kitchener. Behind them is General Joffre and M. Albert Thomas.

15GW912 At the Anglo-French conference at Calais, 6 July, 1915.

French General Joffre and Field Marshal Kitchener, who was opposed to a 'too vigorous' an offensive against the German line, reached a compromise, which was to carry out a 'local offensive on a vigorous scale'. Further, Kitchener agreed to deploy New Army divisions to France. Joffre's plan was for an Anglo-French offensive in the Champagne and Artois areas with the purpose of capturing German railway centres at Attigny and Douai thus forcing a German withdrawal. The ground in the British sector was overlooked by German-held slag heaps and colliery towers and was regarded by some British commanders as unsuitable for an attack. However, they persuaded themselves that the Loos attack could well succeed as the British were intending to use poison gas. It was planned for 25 September.

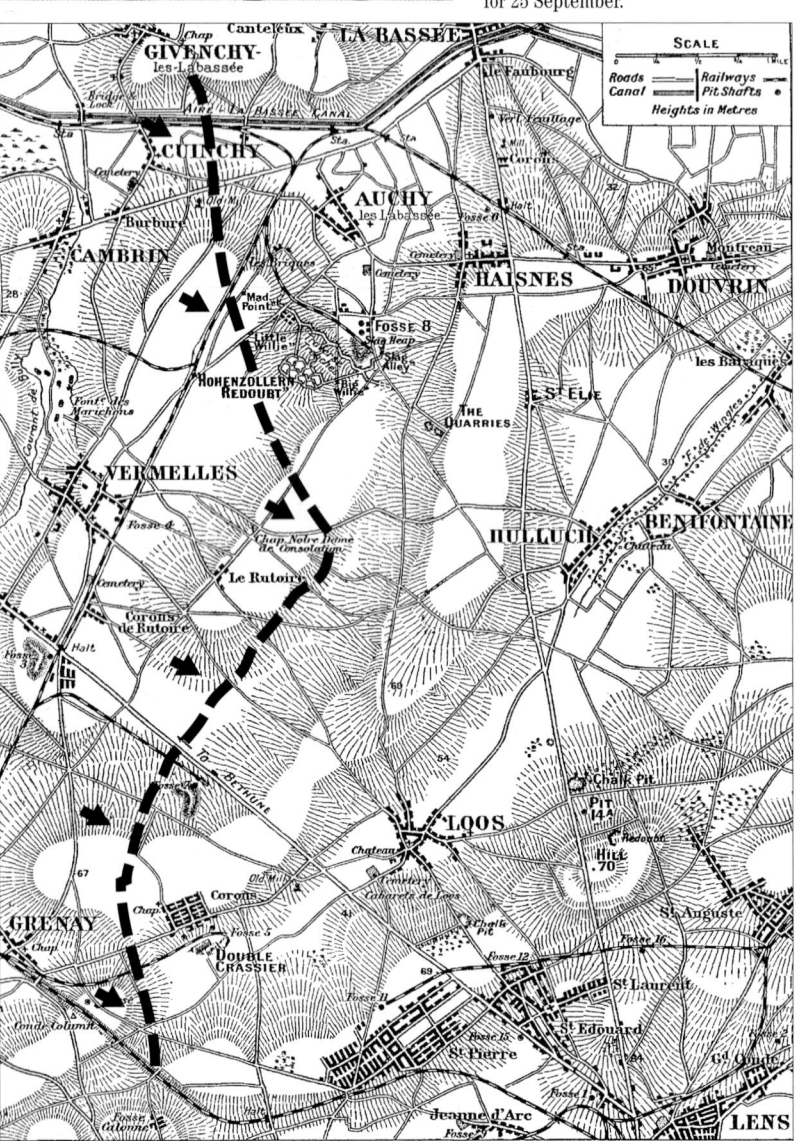

15GW1010 General Sir Douglas Haig, commander of the British First Army, was not too keen on attacking in the area designated because of the flat nature of the land. Also, as gas was to be used for the first time by the British, much depended on the weather. He decided to attack with six infantry divisions.

1915
314

15GW1009 Outside British Army Headquarters in France, Mr Asquith, Prime Minister, with General Joffre and Field Marshal Sir John French. General Joffre's strategy involved the French Army attacking two sectors of the German line. He requested that the British attack in the area of Loos, in support of the French offensive to the north of Arras.

15GW994 Southern section of the British attack in the area of Loos: flat terrain over which the troops were to make their advance with spoil heaps housing German observers and machine guns dominating the ground. Further, it was noted that thick lines of barbed wire ran across the intended line of advance.

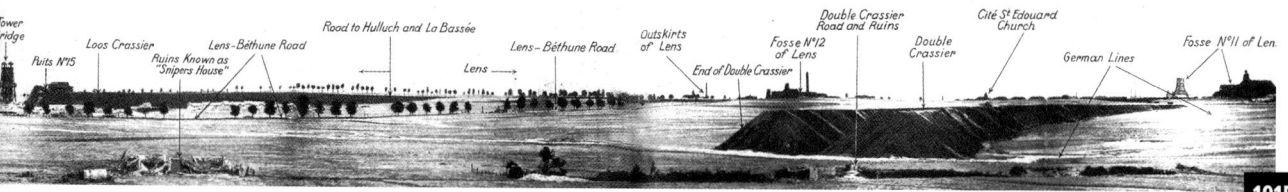

15GW1000 Troops moving up for the attack on the German lines at Loos. London buses are seen in use as transports for troops and supplies.

15GW993 Men of a Scottish battalion marching to the front for the offensive in the Loos sector – August/September 1915.

INDIAN CORPS
Lt-General
Sir C. Anderson

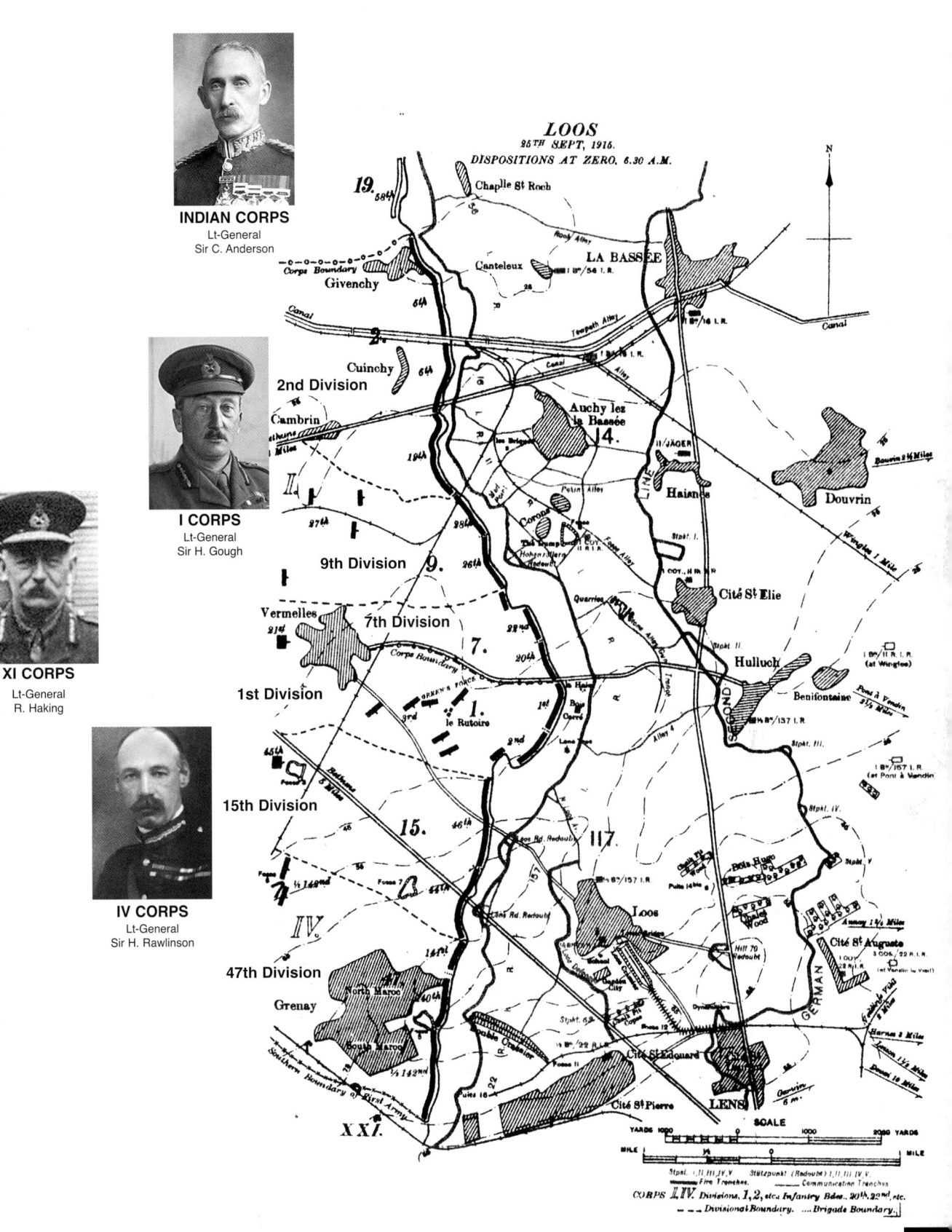

I CORPS
Lt-General
Sir H. Gough

XI CORPS
Lt-General
R. Haking

IV CORPS
Lt-General
Sir H. Rawlinson

LOOS
25TH SEPT. 1915.
DISPOSITIONS AT ZERO, 6.30 A.M.

2nd Division
9th Division
7th Division
1st Division
15th Division
47th Division

1915
317

15GW957 Ruins of Béthune with its belfry; familar to the British troops moving up for the Battle of Loos.

15GW1001 Men of the Gordon Highlanders, 15th (Scottish) Division, in position for the coming attack.

15GW995 The British would be using poison gas for the Battle of Loos.

15GW954 Men of a South Staffordshire battalion in the area opposite the Brickstacks.

15GW1011 A fortified house which has been incorporated into the trench system.

15GW996 British troops training for the attack, becoming used to gas protection.

15GW986 The village of Grenay, behind the British lines, was a mining village in 1915.

15GW978 Two graves in the ruins of the village of Vermelles, each bearing a French memorial wreath.

15GW1008 The Welsh Guards, newly formed in February 1915, moving forward to assemble for the attack on Hill 70.

15GW963 British artillery in action: prior to the attack the German positions were bombarded for four days.

15GW964 North of the La Bassée Canal, looking over No Man's Land; to the right is a railway embankment which had been entrenched as a strongpoint by the Germans. This was named Tortoise Redoubt by the British. For the Battle of Loos this northern part of the attack was undertaken by the British 2nd Division, which straddled the canal.

15GW976 Sector of the Front astride the La Bassée Canal: at the bottom left corner is a string of craters along No Man's Land caused by intense mining activity. The oblong shapes are stacks of bricks where the Germans concealed machine guns and snipers.

British trenches   **No Man's Land**   **German trenches**

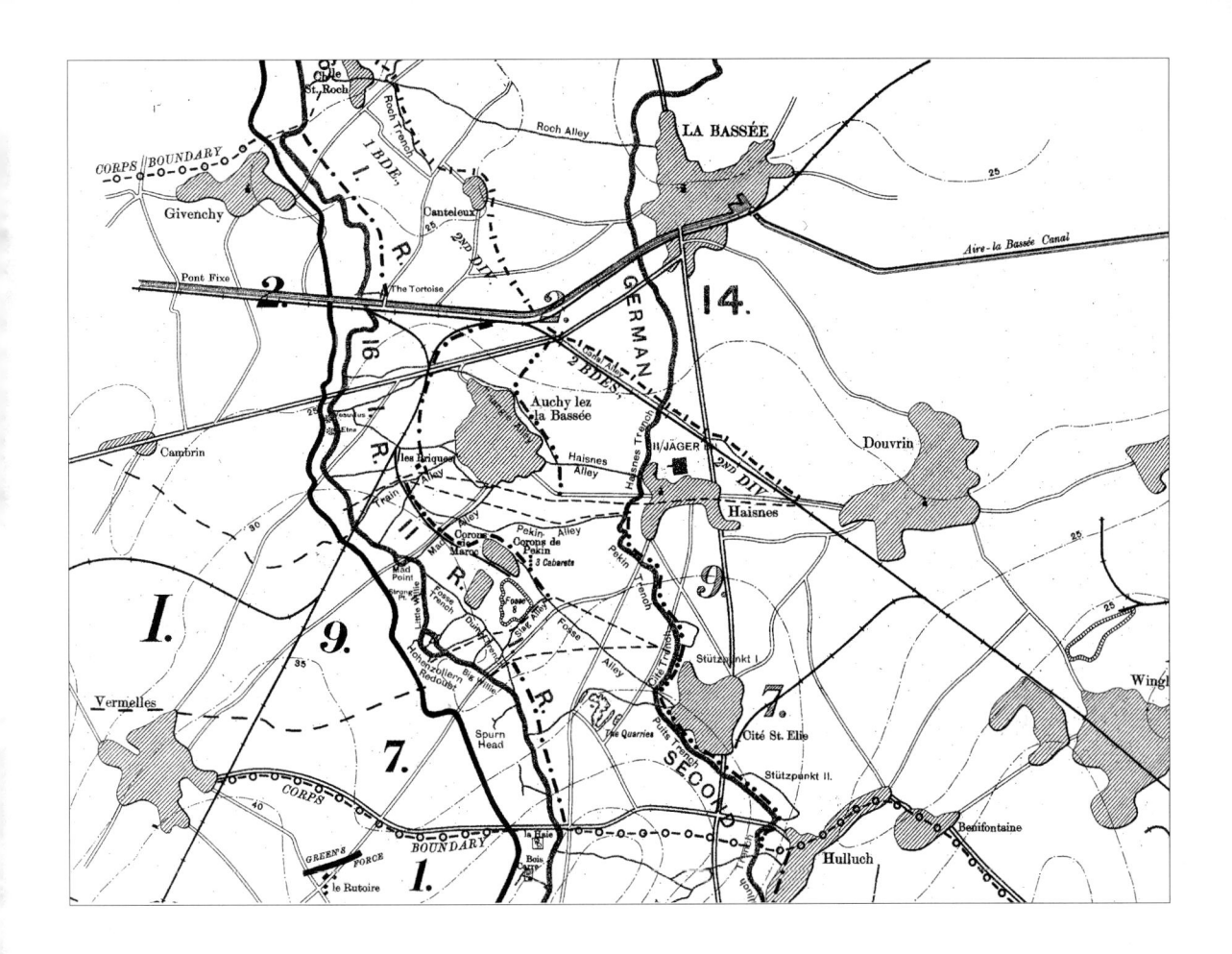

15GW980 The brick stacks immediately behind the German Front Line south of the Bassée Canal, which provided vantage points for artillery spotters, snipers and machine guns.

15GW1013 Ruins of Grenay in 1915, which, at the time of the Battle of Loos, lay close to the Franco-British boundary line. The British 47th Division (IV Corps) occupied it. From here on 25 September the division moved to attack the German position known as the Double Crassier (two spoil stacks); also the Chalk Pit and Loos pit stack. The defending German force was 22 Reserve Infantry Regiment.

15GW1003 The distinctive twin winding gear, nick-named Tower Bridge by the British troops, looms over the occupied houses of Loos; the photograph was taken shortly before the attack.

15GW1004 A trench map showing the German trenches defending the position.

15GW645 A party of B Company, 1st Battalion Scots Guards in Big Willie Trench, Loos, October 1915. This was originally a German trench which led off from the Hohenzollern Redoubt. Three of the men are priming handgrenades.

1915
325

15GW961 The Front south of La Bassée Canal, looking towards the German lines, where the 2nd Division would attack on the morning of 25 September.

15GW982 German machine gun crew posing in the open beside their Maxim 08 which could fire 600 rounds per minute.

15GW962a/b The Front looking towards the colliery associated with Fosse 8, which is on the German Front Line; directly in front and jutting out across No Man's Land is a German strongpoint known as the Hohenzollern Redoubt. Battalions of the British 9th (Scottish) Division were to assault this position.

15GW951 Looking from the British lines towards Vendin-le-Vieil colliery south of Hulluch; the German Second Line ran in front of the coal mine. This area was crossed by the 8/Royal West Kents, 8/Buffs and 9/East Surrey battalions of the 7th Division. They found the wire uncut and were forced to retreat with heavy losses.

15GW959 Royal Welsh Fusiliers moving up for the attack towards the village of Cambrin.

15GW988 Observing the German lines.

15GW969 Scottish troops before the attack; an officer is holding a flare pistol.

15GW973 Explosion from a British-placed mine.

15GW974 View from ground east of Grenay village looking towards the German lines.

15GW985 Germans loading a 75 mm Minenwerfer.

15GW1015 A Royal Field Artillery 18 Pounder Field Gun being loaded by its gun crew.

15GW1014 Fighting underway around the Hohenzollern Redoubt by the 46th (North Midland) Division. This took place in a later phase of the battle, between 13 and 14 October, when the 46th Division fought to recapture the position. In the centre of the picture a pit head gear can be seen – this is Fosse 8. The Redoubt is in front and can be seen marked by sandbags stretching across the landscape.

15GW901 Taken by a soldier of the London Rifle Brigade showing the attack on Loos on 25 September.

1915

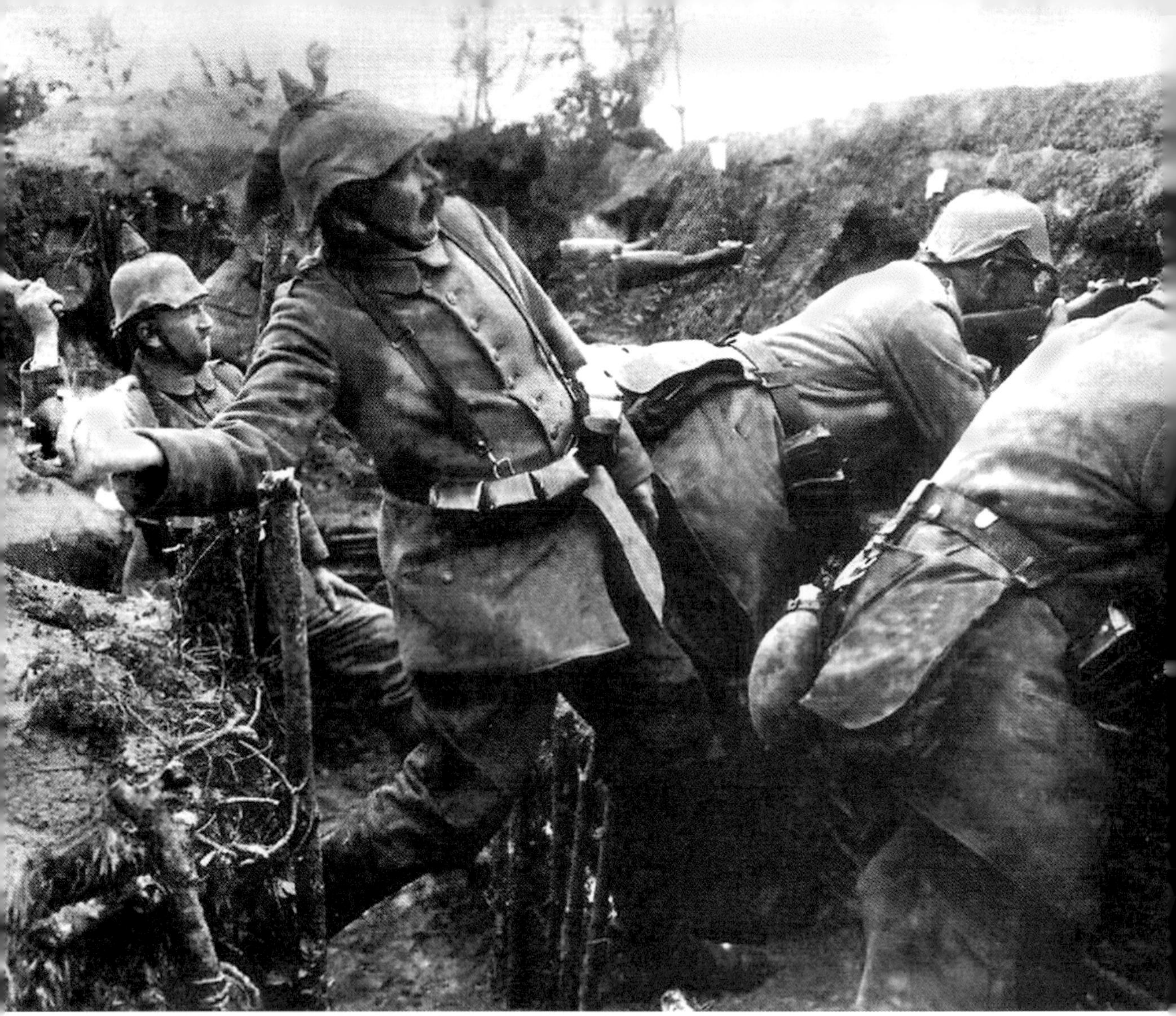

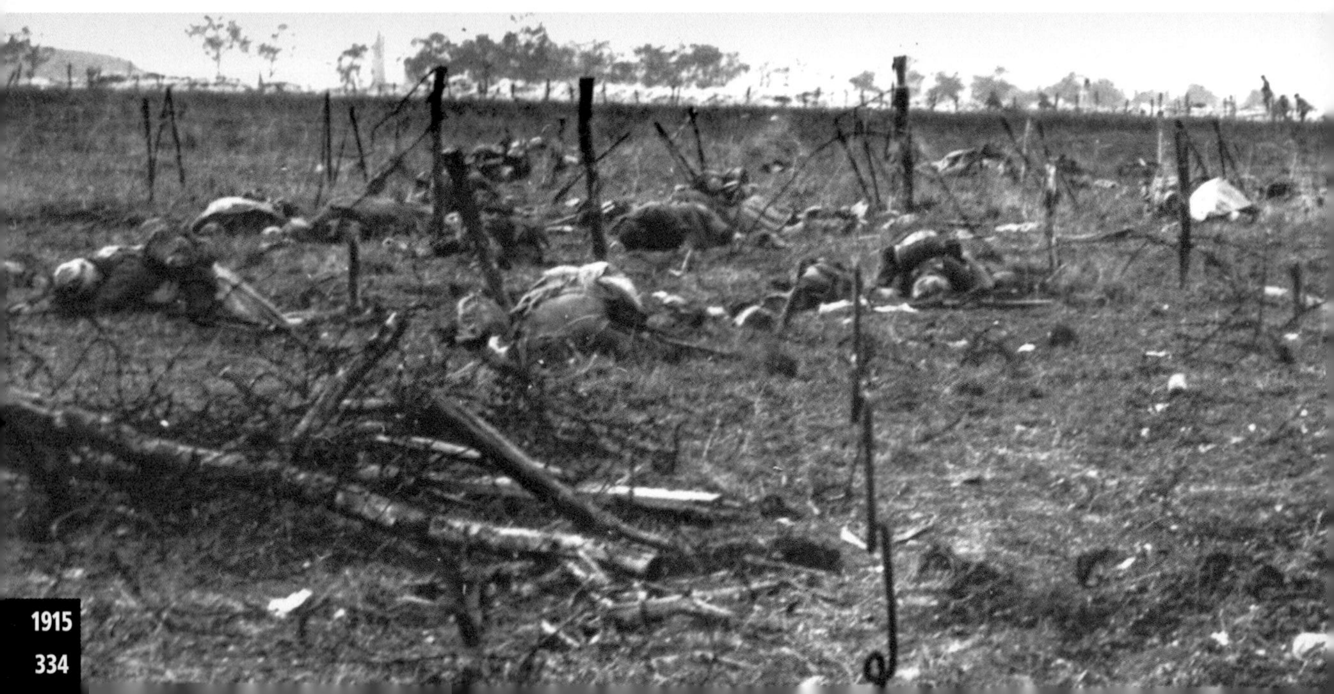

15GW998 An artist's impression of the period depicting the attack by the British 15th Infantry Division.

15GW983 The Germans employed their machine guns with skill, ensuring the best possible results from the weapons' employment.

15GW977 German infantry throwing bombs to repel attackers.

15GW999 Lying among the barbed wire are British dead of 1 Infantry Brigade, 1st Division. Among the attackers on the fortified town of Hulluch were two Kitchener battalions, 8th Battalion Royal Berkshire and 10th Battalion Royal Gloucestershire Regiments.

15GW968 A German machine gun position attacked by men of the 5th Division. Dead of the 2nd Battalion Royal Warwickshire Regiment litter the ground around a gap in the German wire. One man has got through this and been killed close to the trench parapet.

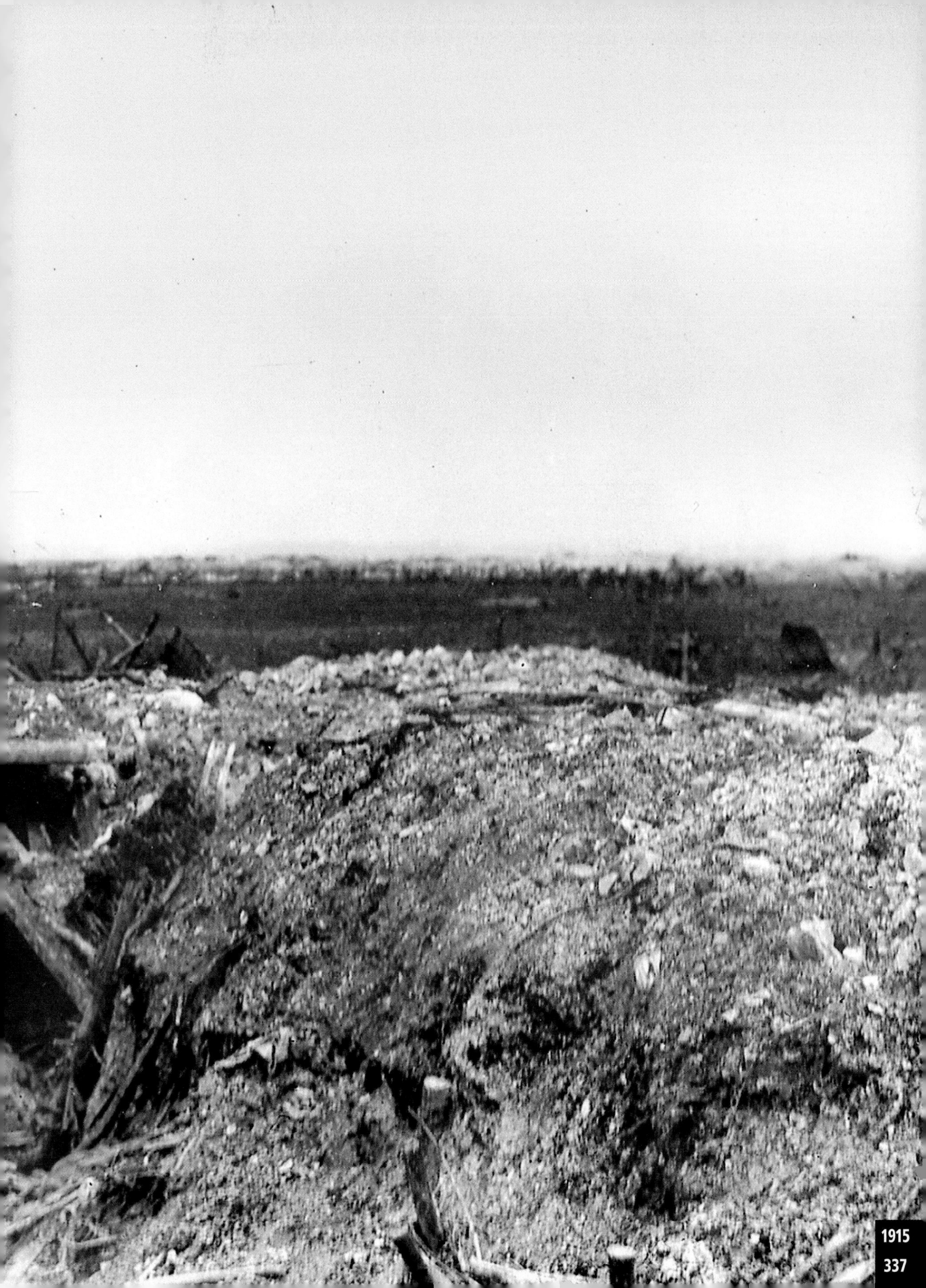

15GW1007 Dead horses and smashed wagons destroyed by German shelling litter the road on either side of a road on Grenay Ridge.

15GW970 A Captured German fire trench.

15GW967 Grenay Ridge, where Royal Artillery horses have been killed by a German artillery barrage.

1915
339

15GW965 German wire entanglements smashed and thrown about but still forming a formidable barrier for attacking infantry.

15GW984 A German 25 cm *Schwerer Minenwerfer,* a heavy trench mortar, being loaded by its crew.

15GW972 A captured trench, where fierce fighting took place.

15GW991 View from the German Front Line across No Man's Land and the direction of the British attack.

15GW992 A captured German position, with dead bodies of the defenders gathered for burial. Judging by the paperwork scattered about they appear to have been searched for useful documents.

15GW990 The bodies of casualties of 7th Battalion, King's Own Scottish Borderers Regiment, 15th Division, killed attacking Loos Road Redoubt, lie among the wire entanglements.

15GW1005 The southern outskirts of Loos, with a colliery spoil heap dominating the area under attack.

1915
345

15GW1006 The 1/7th London Battalion attacked the German strongpoints on the two spoil heaps called the Double Crassier (slag heap) and captured the dugouts and trenches.

15GW1016 The main coal mine around Loos was the one with the twin pit head winding gear, known as London Bridge, which dominated the village; it can be seen through the smoke.

15GW997 An artist's impression of what the British attack looked like. Far too many attackers are depicted as bunched up, shoulder to shoulder.

15GW989 A German 77 mm field gun position captured in the fighting.

15GW1017 An artist's impression of the fighting in the streets of Loos.

15GW1002 Loos shortly after its capture.

15GW1018 A British soldier entering a ruined building to take up a sniping position. His gas hood has been pulled back and is being worn around his cap.

15GW979 Loos Church shortly after the capture of the village and before its tower collapsed.

1915
349

15GW952 British wounded from the Battle of Loos in the main street of Vermelles.

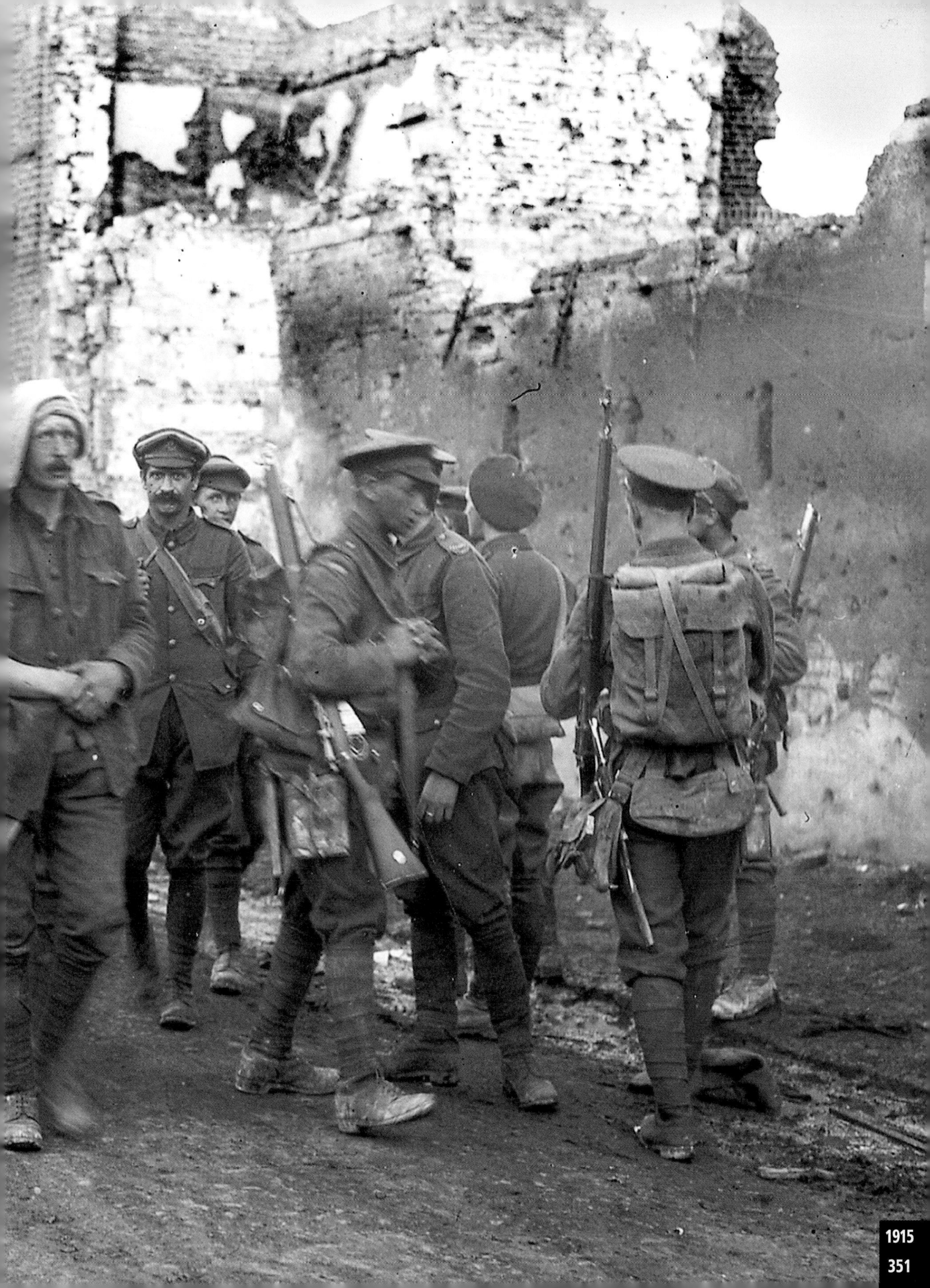

15GW953 British wounded from the Battle of Loos in the main street of Vermelles.

1915
353

15GW1019 A group of English and Scottish soldiers wounded at the fighting round Loos. They wear a label describing the nature of their injuries.

15GW1020 Wounded men on their way by train to the rear. Their clothing is still stained with mud from the battlefield.

15GW1021 Wounded men at a refreshment stop on the way to a Base Hospital. Some men are still wearing their gas hoods.

15GW1043/15GW1044 One of the stone quarries at Hulluch where heavy fighting took place and many German prisoners were taken.

15GW1046/15GW1039/15GW1038 German prisoners captured during the fighting around Loos arriving at Southampton on Wednesday 29 September 1915 and were marched off to a PoW Camp.

Field Marshal Sir John French issued a number of bulletins as the number of prisoners grew; on the 28 September his report stated: 'The number of prisoners exceeds 3,000; the number of machine guns captured is 40. Many more have been destroyed in our bombardment.' The number of divisions initially employed in the fighting was six – attacking three German divisions; casualties were: British 59,2470 and the German losses were estimated at 26,000. Despite the parading of enemy prisoners and displaying of captured equipment the battle was viewed as a failure. The Field Marshal lost support from both the Government and the Army as a result of the British failure at Loos and his ajudged poor handling of his reserve divisions. He was replaced by Haig as Commander of the British Expeditionary Force in December 1915.

1915
357

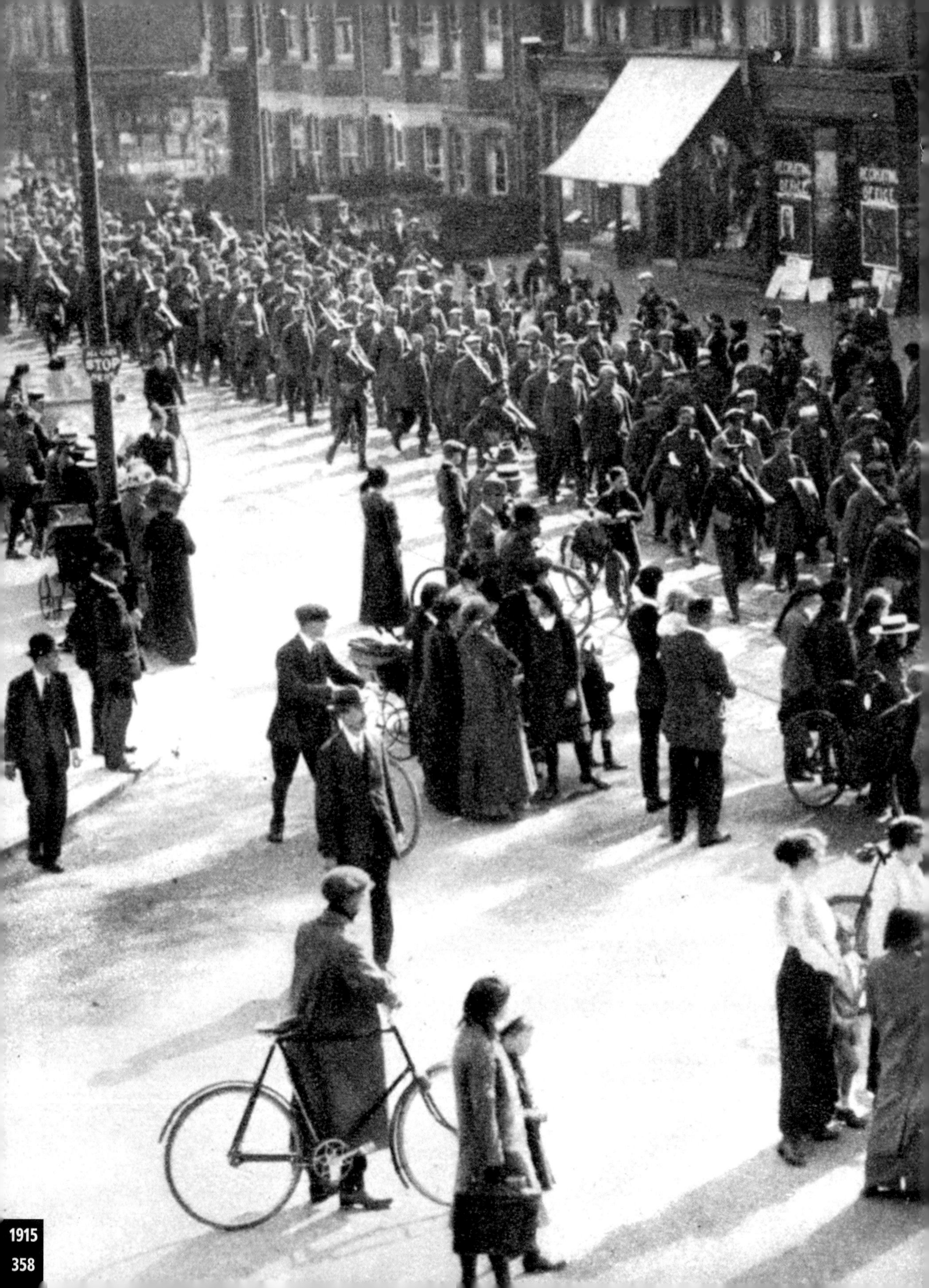
STOP

1915
359

15GW1037 One of the over twenty German guns captured at Loos on board a railway carriage heading for a Channel port and England.

15GW1048 Horse Guards Parade, London, with German field guns captured at Loos on display for the publi.

15GW1022 Trophy from the Battle of Loos, a German field gun captured by the 20th Battalion, London Regiment, was featured in the Lord Mayor's Show, in November 1915.

'THE WHITE COMRADE – "LO, I AM WITH YOU ALWAYS"'
Following the Battle of Loos this painting by G. Hillyard Swinstead was reproduced in the *Illustrated London News* and *The Illustrated War News*, (6 October edition) also it was on display at the War Exhibition at Prince's Skating Rink, London, in 1915. Thus all the death and maiming being suffered was made to appear as divinely sanctioned.

Meanwhile Jesus was brought in to favour all the German soldiers in this postcard depicting a blessing underway:
For Thine is the Kingdom and the power and the glory forever – Amen!

Information used in this chapter was based on the following titles in the **Battleground Europe** series of guide books:
Loos – Hohenzollern and *Loos – Hill 70* by Andrew Rawson
These are available from Pen & Sword History Books Ltd.

Index

1/1/Home Counties Companies, 152
1/1st Gurkhas, 153
1/1st W. Riding Field Companies, 82
1/2nd London, 82
1/2nd Lowland, 82
1/4th Gurkhas, 153
1/5th Royal Scots (TF), 82
1/7th London Battalion, 346
1/Border Regiment, 82
1/Essex Regiment, 82
1/Grenadier Guards, 152
1/Highland LI, 153
1 Infantry Brigade, 335
1/King's Own Scottish Borderers, 82
1/Lancashire Fusiliers, 82
1/Manchester Regiment, 153
1/Northumberland Hussars, 152
1/Royal Dublin Fusiliers, 82
1/Royal Inniskilling Fusiliers, 82
1/Royal Irish Rifles, 152
1/Royal Munster Fusiliers, 82
1/Royal Welsh Fusiliers, 152
1/Sherwood Foresters, 152
1/Sth Staffordshire, 152
1/Worcestershire Regiment, 152
1st (Naval) Brigade, 82
1st (New South Wales) Battalion, 82
1st Australian Brigade, 82
1st Australian Light Horse Regiment, 106
1st Battalion Munster Fusiliers, 82
1st Battalion Border Regiment, 77
1st Canadian Division, 199
2/Bedfordshire Regiment, 152
2/Border Regiment, 152
2/Cameronians Rifles, 152
2/Devonshire Regiment, 152
2/East Lancashire Regiment, 152
2/Gordon Highlanders, 152

2/Hampshire Regiment, 82
2/Highland Signals Service, 152
2/Lincolnshire Regiment, 152
2/Middlesex Regiment, 152
2/Northamptonshire Regiment, 152
2/Rifle Brigade, 152
2/Royal Berkshire Regiment, 152
2/Royal Fusiliers, 82
2/Royal Scots Fusiliers, 152, 158
2/Royal Warwickshire, 152
2/Royal West Surrey Regiment, 152
2/Scots Guards, 152
2/Scottish Rifles, 158
2/South Wales Borderers, 82
2/West Yorkshire Regiment, 152
2/Wiltshire Regiment, 152
2/Yorkshire Regiment, 152
2nd (Naval) Brigade, 82
2nd (New South Wales) Battalion, 82
2nd Australian Brigade, 82
2nd Division, 317, 322, 326
2nd Royal Hampshire, 83
3rd (Australian) Infantry Brigade, 65
3rd (New South Wales) Battalion, 82
3rd (RM) Brigade, 82
3rd Australian Brigade, 82
4/Cameron Highlanders, 152
4/Liverpool Regiment, 153
4/Suffolk Regiment, 153
4/Worcestershire Regiment, 82
4th (Highland) Mountain Brigade, 82
4th (New South Wales) Battalion, 82
4th Australian Brigade, 83
4th Battalion, 13
4th Cavalry Divisional Artillery, 153
4th Colonial Regiment, 83
4.7-inch guns, 153
5th (Victoria) Battalion, 82

5th Battalion Norfolk Regiment, 132
5th Battle Squadron, 8
5th Division, 152, 317, 336, 343
6/Gordon Highlanders, 152
6th (Hood) Battalion, 84
6th (Victoria) Battalion, 82
6th Colonial Regiment, 83
7th (Victoria) Battalion, 82
7th Battalion, 212, 343
7th Division, 317, 324, 328
7th Indian Mountain Artillery Brigade, 83
7th Infantry Division, 152
8/Buffs, 328
8/Royal Scots, 152
8/Royal West Kents, 328
8th (Victoria) Battalion, 82
8th Cyclist Company, 152
8th Infantry Division, 152
9/East Surrey, 328
9th (Queensland) Battalion, 82
9th (Scottish) Division, 327
9th Battalion A.I.F., 76
9th Württemberg, 189
10-inch guns, 19
10th (South Australia) Battalion, 82
11th (Northern) Division, 131
11th (Western Australia) Battalion, 82
12-inch guns, 19
12th (Sth & Wtrn Australia & Tasmania) Battalion, 82
13/London Regiment (TF), 152
13th (New South Wales) Battalion, 83
14th (Victoria) Battalion, 83
14th Siege Battery, 82
15-inch guns, 98
15th (Queensland & Tasmania) Battalion, 83
15th (Scottish) Division, 318
15th Infantry Division, 335

15th Sikhs, 153
16th (South & Western Australia) Battalion, 83
18-pounders, 109, 296–7, 332
20 Brigade, 152
21 Brigade, 152, 154
22 Brigade, 152
23 Brigade, 152
24 Brigade, 152
26th [Jacob's] Battery, 83
29th Division, 65, 82, 102
29th Infantry Division, 71
46th (North Midland) Division, 332
46th Division, 332
47th Division, 317, 324
47th Sikhs, 153
60-pounder, 111, 297
70 Infantry Brigade, 289
77 mm field gun, 22, 56, 62–3, 81, 180, 348
86 Brigade, 82
87 Brigade, 82
88 Brigade, 82–3
90th Heavy Battery, 82
107th Pioneers, 153
127th Infantry Regiment, 189
163 Brigade, 132
175th Regiment Regiment de Marche d'Afrique, 83
460th (Howitzer) Battery, 82

Achi Baba, 98–9, 118
AE2, 34–5
Aegean Sea, 6, 65
Africa, 48
aircraft, 164, 180, 197, 245
airship, 228, 232, 236, 245, 247
Aldershot, 166, 282
Allied line, 114, 182, 199
allies, 19, 43, 51, 65, 91, 95–6, 113, 130, 168, 256, 299
ammunition, 102, 152–3, 215, 298, 303
Anderson, Lt Gen Sir C.A., 153, 317
Anson Battalion, 82-3
ANZAC, 53, 65, 71, 83, 90–1, 103–7, 109, 114, 117, 126, 133, 137, 142, 144
Anzac Cove, 65, 71, 90–1, 105–6, 109, 117, 137, 142
Argyllshire Battery, 82
armies, 151, 215, 250, 267, 357
Arras, 315

artillery, 23, 56–7, 61–2, 76, 78, 82–3, 111, 152–4, 172, 176, 205, 218, 245, 270, 321, 323, 332, 338
Artillery Brigade, 152
Asia, 20, 34, 48, 62, 64–5
Askold, the, 19
Asquith, Prime Minister, 299, 312, 315
Attigny, 314
Aubers Ridge, 146
Australian and New Zealand Army Corps, 71
Australian Brigade, 82–3
Australian Division, 82
Australian Light Horse Regiment, 106
Australians, 65, 82, 109, 114–15

B Beach, 128
B Company, 213, 324
Bailleul, 202
Bareilly Brigade, 153
barges, 82
Barrow, 14
Bassée Canal, 323
battalions, 13, 55, 63, 76–7, 82–4, 132, 146, 154, 161–2, 175, 195–6, 202, 212–18, 226, 265, 272–3, 284, 289–90, 316, 319, 324, 327–8, 335–6, 343, 346, 361
battery, 22, 25, 34–5, 81–3, 111, 152–3
Battle of Dogger Bank, 7, 12, 16
Battle of Loos, 200, 311, 318–19, 322, 324, 350, 352, 361–2
battlecruisers, 12, 14, 17–19, 47
battleships, 8–9, 18, 25, 27, 36, 67, 72, 237
Bavarian Reserve Infantry Regiment, 185
Bayley, Adml Sir Lewis, 8-9
beaches, 37, 65, 70–2, 74–5, 77–8, 80–7, 89, 91–4, 97–8, 103–5, 119–20, 123, 126–30, 140
Beatty, Vice Adml Sir David, 11, 16
Beauchamp, Col Sir Horace, 132
Beck, Capt F, 132–3
Beersheba, 50
Behrens, Herr Georg, 251
Belgian army, 168
Belgium, 146, 178, 248, 251–2, 254–5, 295
Bellewaarde Farm, 208
Béthune, 318
Birdwood, Lt Gen Sir W., 71, 82, 106–7, 136–7

Bissing, Baron von, 254–5
Black Sea, 28, 66
Black Watch, 153–4
Blackader, Brig Gen, 153
Blücher, the, 7, 11–13
boats, 35, 41, 44, 47, 73, 80–2, 84–6, 88–9, 124
    overturned, 58
    rescue, 44
    rowing, 73, 80
    towed, 82
    tug, 41, 78
bodies, 9, 109, 122, 132–3, 158, 200, 342–3
bombardment, 13, 17, 21–3, 26–7, 30, 36–7, 99, 158, 168, 303, 357
bombs, 13, 17–18, 21–8, 30, 36–7, 99, 101, 158, 168, 180, 234, 236, 238–40, 242–7, 284, 303, 321, 335, 357
    dropped, 245
    launch, 284
    mortar, 303
    primitive, 101
Bouvet, the, 18, 26–7
Boyle, Lt Cdr, 34–5
Braemar Castle, 6
Breithaupt, Kapitanleutnant, 245–6
Bridges, Maj Gen W.T., 82
British Army, 48, 94, 118, 121, 125, 177, 182, 215, 270, 285, 303, 315
British Expeditionary Force, 6, 313, 357
British Field Ambulances, 153
British Grand Fleet, 16
British lines, 132, 194, 213, 320, 328
British Mediterranean Expeditionary Force, 65
British troops, 65, 74–5, 80–1, 87, 101, 128–9, 131, 162, 167, 170, 172, 196–7, 206, 210–11, 270, 282, 318, 324, 348
Brock, Capt O. de, 15
Brodie, Cmdr, 34–5, 285
Bromley, Maj, 94
Brooke, Rupert, 65
Brussels, 233, 248–9, 252, 255
Bücking, Rittmeister, 251

Canadian Division, 168, 199
Cape Helles, 36–7, 72, 103
Carden, Vice Adm Sackville Hamilton, 17, 21

Carter, Brig Gen F., 152
casualties, 11, 113, 128, 168, 191, 202, 245, 343, 357
Cattle, Lt, 218
Caucasus front, 17
Cavell, Edith, 248–52, 254–7, 259
Ceylon Planters Rifle Corps, 83
Chatfield, Capt A.E.M., 15
Chatham Battalion, 82
City of London Volunteer Corps, 277
Colver, Lt Harry, 217–18, 225–6
companies, 48, 83–4, 86, 132, 153, 185, 213, 216, 218, 225, 256, 290
Connaught Rangers, 153
Constantinople, 23, 28, 60, 62, 65–7
cordite cartridges, 19
Count Zeppelin, 230, 232
Court of Inquiry, 8
Cowan, Able Seaman John, 9
cruisers, 8, 11–12, 17–18, 23–5, 28
Cunard Line, 42
CXLVII Brigade, 82

Dardanelles, 17–23, 25, 28–9, 32, 34, 65, 69, 104
Davies, Maj Gen Sir F., 152
Deal Battalion, 82
death, 9, 138, 248, 256, 362
Dehra Dun Brigade, 146, 153
Demolition, 17, 29
Denmark, 232
Dent, Capt, 27
Derby Scheme, 262
Dewington Cemetery, 13
divisions, 20, 63, 65, 70, 82–3, 102, 131, 317–18, 322, 324, 326–8, 332, 335–6, 343, 357
Dogger Bank, 7, 10–12, 14, 16
Drake Battalion, 82
Drewry, Midshipman, 84–6
Dublin Fusiliers, 82, 84, 86, 277
dugouts, 106, 131, 176–7, 184, 190, 206, 212, 218–19, 346

E Company, 132
E14, 34–5
E15, 34–5
Edinburgh Castle, 12–13
Egypt, 17, 48, 52–4, 56, 124
El Kantara, 50
Elders & Fyffes Line, 16

Ellison, Maj Gen, 138
engine room, 27
engines, 27, 41, 234, 301
Erdmann, Capt Alexander Karl, 13
Europe, 20, 48, 144, 166, 226, 362
evacuation, 8, 136, 140–3
execution, 251, 255–7, 259
explosions, 36, 43, 98–9, 107, 298, 330

farm buildings, 178, 213, 225
Ferozepore Brigade, 153–4
Field Artillery Brigade, 82
field guns, 22–3, 56, 62–3, 81, 180, 236, 274
First Suez Offensive, 56
Flanders, 203, 212, 215, 226, 238, 285
fleet, 11, 16–17, 19, 21, 39, 66, 70, 245
flotillas, 17
Fort 1, 82
Fort Seddul Bahr, 95
forts, 13, 17–18, 20–8, 30–3, 65, 82, 92, 95, 98–9, 150, 153, 170, 182, 189, 274, 319, 335
Fosse 8, 327, 332
Fox, Col, 217
French, Field Marshal Sir John, 151, 298–9, 313, 315, 357
French troops, 65, 68, 73, 92, 95, 98–9
Front Line, 95, 128–9, 133, 168, 178–9, 197, 215, 217, 220, 222, 225, 323, 327, 342

Gaba Tepe, 37, 65
Gallipoli, 6, 34, 36–7, 47, 61, 64–6, 68–71, 73, 76, 82, 91, 118, 126, 132–3, 136–8, 141, 143–4
Gallipoli landings, 36, 68–9, 138
Gallipoli Peninsula, 37, 64–5, 70, 91, 118, 136, 144
Garhwal Rifles, 153
Garwhal Brigade, 153
gas, 167–8, 198–200, 202–6, 214, 217, 220, 246, 251, 270, 311, 314, 319, 348, 355
Gaulois, the, 26
Geddes, Capt, 83
German Army, 168, 199
Germans, 10–11, 43, 155, 160, 168, 178–9, 189–90, 198–200, 203, 206, 211, 215, 217, 226, 255–6, 270, 311–12, 322, 331, 335

Gibraltar, 182
Godley, Maj Gen Sir, 83
Gordon Highlanders, 318
Govan, 14
Grand Duke Nicholas, 17
Grenay Ridge, 338
Grenfell Maxwell, Lt Gen Sir John, 51
Grimshaw, Cpl, 94
Gulf of Suez, 48
Gully Beach, 119–20, 123, 140
Gully Ravine, 118, 120–3, 125, 144
gun carriage, 13
gunboat, 34
gunfire, 11, 27, 35
guns, 19, 22–3, 25, 27, 29–31, 34–5, 57, 81–4, 87, 98–9, 111–12, 153–4, 161, 236, 245, 261, 274, 297, 299, 315, 322–3, 335, 357, 360
Gurkha Rifles, 153

HAC (Honourable Artillery Company), 172, 176–7, 270
Haig, Gen Sir Douglas, 146, 149, 151, 298, 314, 357
Halsey, Capt, 15
Hamilton, Gen Sir Ian, 17, 64, 70, 82, 132, 138
Hammersley, Maj Gen F., 131
Heavy Battery Ammunition Column, 153
Helles, 65, 144
Henri IV, the, 19
Hersing, Kapitanleutnant, 36–7
Hess, Lt, 220
Hewitt, Capt, 218
Heyworth, Brig Gen F., 152
Hill 60, 167, 189, 192–4, 196–7, 199–200, 202, 226
Hill 70, 321, 362
Hitler, Adolf, 184–7
HMHS *Britannic*, 6
HMS *Agamemnon*, 19
HMS *Albion*, 27
HMS *Amethyst*, 29
HMS *Bayano*, 16
HMS *Beagle*, 36, 76
HMS *Bulldog*, 36
HMS *Chelmer*, 36
HMS *Cornwallis*, 24–5, 143
HMS *Diamond*, 8
HMS *Formidable*, 8–9, 340
HMS *Goliath*, 36

HMS *Hampshire*, 16
HMS *Indomitable*, 10–11, 14
HMS *Irresistible*, 27–8
HMS *Lion*, 10–11, 14–16, 21
HMS *Majestic*, 34–7
HMS *New Zealand*, 15
HMS *Ocean*, 27–8, 42
HMS *Princess Royal*, 14–15
HMS *Queen Elizabeth*, 30
HMS *Tiger*, 15
HMS *Triumph*, 23, 36–7
HMS *Vengeance*, 25, 27
HMS *Viknor*, 10
HMS *Wear*, 27
Hohenzollern, 324, 327, 332, 362
Honigmann, Leutnant, 251
Honourable Artillery Company *see* HAC
Hood Battalion, 82
hospital ship, 6, 65
hospitals, 9, 248
Howe Battalion, 82
Howitzer Brigade, 153
howitzers, 31, 62, 82–3, 153
Huguet, Gen, 313
Hulluch, 335, 356
Huns, 6, 207
Hunter-Weston, Maj Gen Sir, 71, 82, 102
Hutchins, Maj, 83
Hütten, Leutnant, 251

I (New South Wales) Field Artillery Brigade, 82
I Portsmouth Battalion, 82
II (Victoria) Field Artillery Brigade, 82
III (Queensland) Field Artillery Brigade, 82
Incendiary, 240, 242
Indian Army, 50, 279
Indian Corps, 150, 153, 317
Indian Field Ambulances, 153
Indian Mountain Artillery Brigade, 83
Indian troops, 142, 145, 147–8, 154–5
International Trench, 217, 222, 226
invasion, 47, 60, 66, 70, 82, 88, 96, 118, 126–7
Iron Cross, 187, 241
Istanbul, 23, 28
IV Brigade, 153
IV Corps, 317, 324
IX Brigade, 153

Jacob, Brig Gen C.W., 83, 153
Jodhpur Lancers, 149
Joffre, Gen, 149, 313–15
Johnson, Alderman Sir Charles, 280
Johnson, Capt, 213
Jullundur Brigade, 153

Kaiser Wilhelm II, 180
Kataib-el-Kheil, 50
Keary, Lt Gen Sir H.D., 153
Keneally, L/Cpl, 94
Kephez Point, 34
Kilid Bahr, 20
Kilitbahir, 65
killed, 9, 29, 34, 37, 45, 84, 86, 107, 158, 161, 164, 199, 217, 238–9, 242, 245–7, 336, 338, 343
King Edward VII, 132
King George V, 132, 262
King George's Own Sappers, 153
King's Own Royal (Lancasters) Regiment, 195
Kitchener, Field Marshal, 70, 136–7, 272–3, 284, 289, 298–9, 312–14, 335
Krupp guns, 25, 56, 62, 81
Kum Kale, 25, 32, 65

La Bassée Canal, 322, 326
Lahore Division, 153
Lahore Divisional Ammunition Column, 153
Lahore Signal Company, 153
Lake Constance, 228–9, 231
Lancashire Fusiliers, 82, 88
land, 28, 74, 82, 84, 114, 118, 126, 178, 192, 216, 220, 228, 314, 322, 327, 342
landings, 30, 32, 34, 47, 52, 63, 65–6, 70, 72, 80–2, 84–5, 90–2, 96, 99–101, 103, 118, 126–7, 144, 236
Langemark, 200
Lanz minenwerfer, 226
Lawford, Brig Gen, 152
Leicestershire Regiment, 153
Lemnos, 34, 68
lifeboats, 44–5, 85
Liman von Sanders, Gen Otto, 56, 63
Liverpool, 10, 40, 153, 208, 245
Liverpool Scottish, 208
Lloyd George, David, 298–9
London, 227, 243, 245–6, 256, 262, 266–7, 360, 362

London Regiment, 361
London Rifle Brigade, 332
London Territorials, 259, 284
London Volunteer Corps, 277
Lone Pine, 108–9
Long Lee Enfield, 175
Loos, 189, 200, 256, 311–62
Lord Derby, 262, 264
Louvain, 254
Loxley, Capt, 8
Loyal North Lancashire Regiment, 290
Lumb, Sgt Maj, 213
LZ 37, 246–7
LZ1, 228–9
LZ2, 228
LZ3, 228, 230–1
LZ4, 228

machine gun, 72, 83–4, 86–7, 112, 155, 161, 163, 182, 210, 226, 287, 315, 322–3, 327, 335–6, 357
Malleson, Midshipman, 84–6
Mallinson, Capt, 213
Malta, 21
Maple Copse, 176
marines, 17, 28–9, 32–4, 42, 59
Martinique, 199
Masnou, Gen, 83
Masque Robert, 204
Masque Vanquit, 204
Mathy, Kapitanleutnant, 235
Mediterranean Expeditionary Force, 70, 82, 138
Meerut Division, 153
Meerut Signal Company, 153
Menin Gate, 170–1
Middlesex Regiment, 289
Minenwerfer, 331
mines, 6, 10, 18, 20–1, 26–8, 34, 71, 74–5, 77, 153, 208, 226, 328, 330–1, 340, 346
minesweepers, 21, 74–5, 77
Ministry of Munitions, 299
Mobile Veterinary Sections, 152
Monro, Gen, 136, 138
Moritz von Bissing, Generaloberst, 254
Morto Bay, 36
Motor Maxim Squadron, 82
Mount Dardanos, 26
Mountain Brigade, 82
mules, 52, 57, 121, 292
Munsters, 84

Nagara, 29
Napier's Rifles, 153
National Guard, 277, 279–81
Naval Observation Station, 103
Neuve Chapelle, 145–6, 148, 154–8, 160–6, 298
New Zealand, 15, 52–5, 65, 71, 82–3, 91, 105
New Zealand Brigade, 52, 55, 83
New Zealand Engineers, 83
Newman, Sgt, 279
Nicholson, Rear Adml, 69, 103
Nightingale, Capt, 86
No Man's Land, 114, 178, 192, 216, 220, 322, 327, 342
Norfolk Regiment, 132–3, 239
North Sea, 9, 11, 16
North Staffordshire Regiment, 290
nurses, 249, 254, 256

officers, 8, 10, 27, 37, 62–3, 71, 107, 120, 132, 161, 176, 180, 187, 190, 212–13, 217, 226, 241, 274, 279, 330
operations, 32, 182
Ormsby-Johnson, Flag-Lt Lionel S., 21
Ottomans, 21, 23–8, 47–8, 56, 63, 65–7

Paris, Maj Gen A., 82
Parkinson, Capt, 85, 226
Parry-Smith, Capt, 213, 225
Pelly, Capt H.B., 15
Pera, 67
periscope, 36–7, 173, 177, 225
pickelhaube, 184
Pilgrim Route, 50
Pinney, Brig Gen, 152
Pioneers, 152–3
Plain of Esdraelon, 51
Plymouth Battalion, 82
poison, 34, 168, 198–9, 203–4, 206, 311, 314, 319
Port Said, 48, 56
Port Tawfiq, 48
Portland, 8–9
Portugal, 285
Portuguese Army, 285
President Wilson, 45
prisoners, 34, 58–9, 124, 132, 141, 160, 162, 166, 200, 356–7
propaganda, 43, 45, 200, 255–6

Quien, Gaston, 251

Rajah of Rutlam, 148–9
Rathgen, Prof., 251
Rawlinson, Sir Henry, 152
recruiting, 256, 259, 262, 264, 266–7
regiment, 55, 77, 82–3, 106, 132, 160–2, 175, 182, 185, 187, 189, 195, 197, 213–18, 226, 239, 265, 272, 289–90, 324, 335–6, 343, 361
reinforcements, 90, 96, 141
Repington, Charles, 298
Reserve Infantry Regiment, 324
RFA (Royal Field Artillery), 82, 152–3, 245, 332
Richards, Sgt, 94
Rideal, Capt, 226
rifles, 63, 83, 86, 102, 107, 115, 129, 140, 152–4, 158, 172, 175, 216, 225, 277, 283–6, 293, 332
Ritter von Hipper, Franz, 11
River Clyde, 72, 82–7, 92–3, 98–9
River Yser, 168
RMS *Hesperian*, 38
RMS *Lusitania*, 38, 40–6, 254
Roebeck, Adml de, 21, 64, 69
Ross & Cromarty Battery, 82
Rosyth, 14
Royal Army Medical Corps Field Hospital, 294
Royal Artillery, 111, 338
Royal Australian Navy, 34
Royal Dublin Fusiliers, 82–3
Royal Engineers, 82, 100–1
Royal Field Artillery, 82, 152–3, 245, 332
  see also RFA
Royal Flying Corps, 245
Royal Fusiliers, 121, 273
Royal Gloucestershire Regiment, 272, 335
Royal Hampshires, 83
Royal Horse Artillery, 82
Royal Irish Fusiliers, 134
Royal Munster Fusiliers, 82–3
Royal Naval Air Service, 82
Royal Naval Division, 82–4, 266
Royal Navy, 7–9, 11–12, 19, 24, 34, 36, 58, 65–6, 92
Royal Scots, 13, 82, 152, 158
Royal Welsh Fusiliers, 328
Royal West Kents, 193, 328

sailors, 9–13, 28–9, 35, 40, 43, 48, 65
salient, 168, 172–3, 175, 195, 198–9, 206, 214–15, 218
sally ports, 72, 82, 84
Salonica, 6
Samson, Seaman George, 84–5
Samson, Wing Cdr C.R., 66, 84, 86
Sanctuary Wood, 176–7, 210, 226
sandbags, 84, 147, 176, 178, 182, 192, 220, 225, 332
Sandringham Company, 133
Scarborough, 13
Schacht, Dr, 251
Schneider, Cmdr R, 8–9
School of Musketry, 261
Schotthöfer, Herr, 251
Schwerer Minenwerfer, 340
Schwieger, Kapitanleutnant W., 43
Scinde Rifles, 153
Scotland, 14, 16, 84
Scottish battalion, 196, 316
Scottish Borderers, 82, 212, 343
Scottish regiment, 197, 330
Sea of Marmara, 34
Second Battle of Krithia, 84
Second Battle of Ypres, 167–8, 199
Second World War, 6, 270
Sedd el Bahr, 29–30, 32–3, 82, 92, 99
shells, 18–19, 24–5, 27–31, 71, 92, 106–7, 140, 168, 177, 200, 208, 213, 261, 298, 308, 338
shelters, 118, 120, 175
ships, 8–9, 11–12, 14–15, 17–19, 25, 27–9, 36, 39–43, 48–9, 66–7, 77, 84–5, 92, 98, 122–4, 144
  allied, 25
  bombarding, 28
  fast fighting, 14
  hospital, 6
  non-military, 43
  transport, 34
shore, 17, 30, 36–7, 71–4, 82, 84–6, 88, 117
Short Lee Enfield, 175, 283–5
Signals Company Medical Unit, 152
Sikh Pioneers, 153
Sinai Desert, 57
Singh, Lt Gen Sir Pertab, 148–9
sinking, 6–9, 11–13, 16–17, 27, 34, 36, 38, 42–4, 254
Sirhind Brigade, 153

Skyros, 65
Smith, Samuel, 239, 242
SMS *Barbaros Heyreddin*, 67
SMS *Blücher*, 7, 11–13
SMS *Breslau*, 66–7
SMS *Derfflinger*, 14
SMS *Kurfürst Friedrich Wilhelm*, 66–7
snipers, 49, 86–7, 107, 112, 117, 129, 137, 173, 207, 322–3, 348
soldiers, 35, 60, 63, 65, 70–1, 74–5, 83–4, 87, 106–7, 112–15, 123, 126–7, 131–2, 147, 156, 161, 165, 180, 197, 199–200, 205–6, 215, 239, 244, 246, 248, 251–2, 254, 256, 270, 273, 281, 286, 332, 354, 362
South Staffordshire Battalion, 319
Southey, Brig Gen, 153
Sportsman's Battalion, 273
squadron, 8, 10–12, 14, 17–18, 82
SS *Nile*, 74
SS *River Clyde*, 72, 83–7
St Albans, 272
St Eloi, 172, 177
St Floris, 146
St Giles Prison, 252
St Julien, 206
St Pancras, 280
steamer, 10, 49
Stoker, Lt Henry, 34–5
Stopford, Lt Gen Sir F., 126
straits, 17–18, 20–2, 34, 65
Strickland, Brig Gen E., 153
Stubbs, Sgt, 94
Suandere, 26
submarines, 8–9, 34–9, 42–3, 45
Sudan, 48
Suez Canal, 48–51, 56–7, 59
Suffren, the, 26
Suvla, 116, 126–9, 132, 136–7, 143–4

Taylor, Martha, 239
Tenedos, 33
Thomas, Albert, 313
Tisdall, Lt, 84–5
Tizzard, Lt Col, 82
Tommies, 139, 194, 202
Topaze, 8
torpedo, 6–9, 16, 34, 36–7, 39, 42–3
Tortoise Redoubt, 322
training, 277, 282, 295–6, 299
transport, 6, 34, 72, 74, 76, 126, 129, 153, 228, 230, 293, 316
trenches, 64, 95, 103, 107–9, 111, 128–9, 131, 140–1, 146–7, 154–5, 161, 164–5, 172, 176–7, 179, 182, 189–90, 195, 198–200, 208, 210–11, 213, 215, 217–18, 220–2, 226, 279, 281, 283–5, 303, 322, 324, 336, 338, 340–1, 346
Treutler, Herr, 251
Turkey, 17, 23, 28, 34, 60, 133
Turks, 17, 47, 49–51, 62–3, 66, 86, 113–15, 140, 143
Turner, William Thomas, 42, 45
Tyrwhitt, Commodore, 15

U-20, 38–9, 43, 45
U-21, 9, 36–7
U-24, 8–9
U-27, 16
Universities and Public Schools Brigade, 295
University and Public Schools Ambulance Corps, 292
Unwin, Cmdr, 84–6
Urabi Revolt, 48

V Beach, 82–3, 86, 92
V Brigade, 152–3
V Brigade Ammunition Column, 153
Vaughan's Rifles, 153
Vermelles, 320, 350, 352
vessel, 34, 43, 79, 82
Vice Adml Beatty's flagship, 16
Victoria Cross, 34, 84, 86, 247, 279
Victoria Luise, the, 230
victory, 11, 35
volunteers, 147, 262, 264, 308

W Beach, 37, 94
W Company, 82–3
Walker, Brig Gen, 153
Warneford, Flt Sub-Lt, 247
Watts, Brig Gen, 152
Welsh Guards, 321
West Riding Field Engineers, 83
Western Front, 150, 199
Weston, Hunter, 71
Wildes Rifles, 153–4
Willcocks, Sir James, 153
Williams, Able Seaman W., 84–6
Willis, Capt, 94, 213
wire, barbed, 122, 147, 155, 161, 182, 190, 219, 315, 328, 335, 343

Wodehouse, Lt Col, 161
Worcestershire Regiment, 82, 160–2
wounded, 6, 29, 84–6, 94, 122–5, 128, 165, 200, 202, 256, 292–5, 350, 352, 354–5

X Company, 82–3
XI Brigade, 153
XIII Brigade, 153
XV Brigade, 82
XVII Brigade, 82
XVIII Brigade, 153
XXXIII Artillery Brigade, 152
XXXVII Brigade, 152
XXXVIII Brigade, 152
XLIII Brigade, 153
XLV Brigade, 152

Y Batteries, 82
Y Company, 82–3
Yeni Shehr, 32
Yeomanry, 131
York and Lancaster Regiment, 175, 213–18, 220–1, 226
Ypres, 146, 167–226, 311
Yser, 168, 215–18, 220–1

Z Battery, 152
Z Company, 82–3
Zeppelins, 227–60
Zillebeke, 178